To John.

with our

You

Love
Dave & Joy.

BATH:

Valley of the Sacred Spring

Kim Green

BATH: *Valley of the Sacred Spring*

First published in 2004
by Second Nature Press
of Bath

Photography & Book Design: Kim Green
Origination & Cover Design: Bob Wilson
Printed: The Cromwell Press

ISBN: 0-9545175-0-4

BATH:

Valley of the Sacred Spring

Kim Green

For my daughter Holly with all my love.

Acknowledgements

The author would like to thank the following for their kind permission to reproduce illustrations:

The Victoria Art Gallery Bath
For details from the portraits of Richard Nash (p.55) and Ralph Allen (p.60).
Barry Cunliffe
For the original line drawing of the Lansdown sun disc (p.11).
The British Museum Department of Prints and Drawings
For Thomas Johnson's illustration of the King's Bath (p.46).
The Royal National Hospital for Rheumatic Diseases
For William Hoare's painting of Dr. Oliver at the Royal Mineral Hospital (p.86).
Bath and North East Somerset Council – Bath Central Library
For the illustration based on John Speed's map of Bath 1610 (p.50).
The Bath Preservation Trust
For the detail of John Wood from William Hoare's painting,
'The Four Worthies' (p.61).

All other photographs are copyright of the author.

The extract from Louie Stride's 'Memoirs of a street Urchin' (p.109), is reproduced with the kind permission of Bath University Press.
The extract from James Lees-Milne's biography of William Beckford (p.104) is reproduced with the kind permission of Century Publishing.

I would like to thank Colin Johnstone at the Bath Archive Office for his much valued assistance in tracking down historical sources; Peter Davenport of the Bath Archaeological Trust for details of the Cross Bath excavations, and staff at the Roman Baths and the Abbey Vaults Museum.
Additional thanks to Keith Green for casting an eye over the manuscript; to Philippa for making it happen, and to Professor Ivan and Margaret Roitt for their support and encouragement over many years.
Every effort has been made to acknowledge sources and secure permission from copyright owners. The author offers sincere apologies for any oversights. I am entirely responsible for any historical errors.

CONTENTS

Contents   Page

BATH: *Valley of the Sacred Spring*

THE FIRST PILGRIM

The dawn air is sharp with frost on the forest hillslope where the hunter wakes from an uneasy sleep, still clutching the flint-headed spear he has not once released from his grip throughout the long winter night. Pulling the rough hide covering tight up to his chin, he casts a wary eye about him. The dim shapes glimpsed through the dying firelight of his makeshift camp have retreated once more into the forest, and the cries of unfamiliar creatures have ceased.

Stiffly rising from his bed of earth and pine needles, the hunter gathers together what is left of yesterday's meagre catch, and the few roots, nuts and berries he has been able to forage along the margins of the river valley. Then, kicking over the ashes of the fire, he begins his slow descent to the river bank where, among the reed-mace and willow, he has hidden the dug-out canoe which will carry him back downstream to the tribe's winter camp.

But as he makes his way through the trees, something catches his eye in the valley below. On the other side of the river he can make out an area where the frost has not settled, and where dense white clouds are billowing up into the chill morning air. Observing his own warm breath misting in the freezing air, the hunter stops dead in his tracks. What he is witnessing can surely have only one explanation: here must dwell a giant – one of the underworld gods who created the trees and streams upon which his own existence depends. Perhaps in some way he has displeased the guardians of this unfamiliar domain and must now make penitence by offering back the few fish he has taken from the river. Mustering as much courage as he is able, the hunter continues his journey down to the reed beds, his heart beating wildly.

Pushing the canoe out into the open river and steering his way upstream, the hunter notices the banks on the north side of the river are marshier. Rivulets of steaming water gush from the tangled vegetation, making them too unsteady to moor his boat safely. But a little further upstream he discovers a narrower point in the river, easily forded and where the banks are firmer. The crossing offers a safer approach and a quicker retreat should the gods be further angered at his intrusion. Hauling his dugout onto the gravel bank, he sets off in the direction of the white mists – emboldened a little now by the faint hope that he may have been called to this earth magic for some special purpose.

A short distance from the river, a clearing in the trees reveals a steaming swamp where hot bubbling water gushes from the ground. The surrounding rocks and vegetation are stained blood-red: the blood of some animal – or perhaps human sacrifice. The sight is both awe-inspiring and terrifying; the silence in the glade, eerie and otherworldly. Courage fails him at last and the first pilgrim to the Valley of the Sacred Spring sinks to his knees, overwhelmed, in a spontaneous act of reverence and propitiation.

THE GEOLOGY OF THE HOT SPRINGS

The three hot springs to which the city of Bath owes its existence are a unique phenomenon in the English landscape. Yet there are few visible clues in the encircling Cotswold hillsides, or in the Avon River valley which snakes its way between them, to suggest why they should occur here and nowhere else in Britain.

It can be no wonder that the springs in their primeval state, presented such a mysterious and awesome sight to our distant ancestors, so intimately connected as they were to the phenomena of the natural world and the gods who they believed created them.

Today we may understand much more about how the springs came to exist, yet our scientific knowledge takes away none of their fascination. In fact in some ways the geological explanations are as fantastic and unlikely as are the myths and legends that surround their origins.

The hot mineral springs of Bath that still gush from the earth at a rate of a quarter of a million gallons a day, at an average temperature of around 45 degrees C, have their probable origins in a period of intense mountain building which occurred in central Europe approximately 380 million years ago. The cataclysmic forces unleashed by this geological upheaval sent shock waves west into southern Britain, resulting in the folding and lifting of the Carboniferous limestone strata in the area we now know as North Somerset. The horizontal layers of limestone were forced upwards into giant waves, exposing the fractured bedding planes. To the north of these limestone crests, which now outcrop as the Mendip Hills, the strata were depressed into a deep trough, rising again close to Bath. These layers are now buried beneath later geological deposits such as the Jurassic oolitic limestone which forms the southern-most tip of the Cotswolds and from which the Georgian city of Bath is built. Between these two ranges of hills, the River Avon carved out a wide, steep-sided valley on its journey west to the sea.

Over millions of years the porous Carboniferous limestone of the Mendips was further eroded by rains seeping down through the sloping bedding planes towards the heat of the earth's core. Faultlines in the strata then allowed the water, heated to temperatures of between 64C and 96C – and under enormous pressure – to be forced up through the succeeding deposits of rock, and back towards the surface. Here it burst through fissures in the top layers of clay, close to the banks of the River Avon – 10,000 years after it began its journey, and many miles north of where it first fell as rain on the Mendip Hills.

On its long voyage underground, the thermal waters have accumulated the dissolved residues of 43 different minerals, including the oxidised iron salts which are responsible for the ochre discolouring of rock and vegetation that must once have symbolised, in the minds of our hunting ancestors, the blood of slaughtered animals. One cannot help but wonder if they would have been any less astonished had they known of the waters natural origins.

THE STONE CIRCLES OF STANTON DREW

With the introduction of farming, mankind had at last learned to harness nature to its own ends, and soon the collective human energies required to achieve this were also being directed towards the creation of the most spectacular of prehistoric man's endeavours: the giant stone circles such as those at Stonehenge and Avebury.

These extraordinary megalithic monuments were probably begun during the late Neolithic/early Bronze Age, around 3000-2000 BC. The remains of one of them survive a few miles from Bath, at Stanton Drew.

The creation of stone circles is believed to have been linked to major astronomical events, particularly the movements of the sun and the moon, and although their exact function is still uncertain, it seems probable that they fulfilled some purpose as places of assembly where the calendrical changes associated with the cycles of the farming year were celebrated in ritual ceremonies. The sites at Stonehenge, Avebury and Stanton Drew, were also to be identified with the later ceremonies of the Druids, the powerful priesthood of the Celtic peoples who would comprise the next significant migrations to these shores.

Standing Stone from the outer circle at Stanton Drew, near Bath.
The great stone circles of Stonehenge and Stanton Drew had probably reached the final stages of their completion around 1500 BC. Their construction and alignment, based on sophisticated astronomical observation of the sun and moon, were, together with a less certain connection with later Druid ceremony, to exert a powerful influence on the prime architect of Georgian Bath, John Wood.

THE NEOLITHIC PERIOD AND THE STONE AGE

The warmer climate of the post-glacial period, around 10,000 years ago, saw the retreat of the cold-tolerant pine forests and the colonisation of the Avon Valley hill-slopes by the now familiar deciduous tree species such as lime, beech, oak, hazel and alder. Man's existence, on the other hand, had probably altered little throughout the long millennia of the Early and Middle Stone Ages. Still an essentially nomadic hunter-gatherer, his own environmental impact on the valley is likely to have been minimal.

But with the arrival of farming peoples from mainland Europe in the late Neolithic Period, around 4000 BC, the landscape was to undergo a gradual, yet dramatic, transformation. The cultivation of crops and the domestication of sheep and cattle, witnessed the forest clearance of hilltops and the establishment of settled communities. Evidence of such defended hill settlements has been identified on the outskirts of the present-day city at Bathampton and Solsbury Hill.

Further dramatic developments were to follow in the second millennium BC, with the introduction of first copper, then bronze, technology. The production of the new tools and weapons – which depended on a regional availability of resources – was to break down the relative self-sufficiency of the older Stone Age cultures and intensify the need for trade links between tribes. With the production of surplus and luxury commodities such as pottery, woven goods and jewellery made possible, the River Avon and the ancient limestone track, the Jurassic Way, became ever more vital trade and communication routes. Tin from Cornwall, and lead from the Mendip Hills would almost certainly have passed through the valley on its way to Wessex, the Thames Valley and mainland Europe.

In the last centuries of the first millennium BC the new economies opened the way to political control of access to, and distribution of, goods and materials. Britain became part of a trade network which may well have encompassed the entire Classical World. It was only a matter of time before the island's mineral wealth attracted the territorial ambitions of the Roman Empire. Someday it would attempt to wrest control of these resources from the regional warrior aristocracies in the south of the country. The hot springs of the Avon River Valley would play a unique part in this drama.

THE LANSDOWN SUN-DISC

The hillside burial sites of the Bronze Age known as round barrows are among the few sources of archaeological record of the pre-Iron Age landscape around Bath, yet they offer a fascinating insight into the growing sophistication of prehistoric cultures. Excavations of several of these tumuli have revealed a number of objects buried with the dead, including hand-made pottery, jewellery and bronze daggers.

The most impressive of these finds is a gilded bronze 'sun-disc', retrieved, in very fragile condition, from one of two round barrows excavated by local antiquarians in 1905 on the slopes of Lansdown, north of the hot springs. The disc, approximately six inches in diameter, is believed to have dated from the period around 1400-1000 BC and formed part of the grave-goods marking the final resting-place of what may have been a Bronze Age chieftain.

The sun symbol itself would re-occur many times, in different guises, in the Roman religious sanctuary dedicated to Sulis Minerva constructed around the site of the Sacred Spring.

THE GROVE

That the Romans respected and feared the mysterious places associated with the power of the Druids is powerfully conveyed in the description of a sacred grove in Southern Gaul by the Roman poet Lucan (39-65 AD), from his epic poem *Pharsalia*:

A grove there was, untouched by men's hands from ancient times, whose interlacing boughs enclosed a space of darkness and cold shade, and banished the sunlight from above...gods were worshipped there with savage rites, the altars were heaped with hideous offerings, and every tree was sprinkled with human gore. On those boughs...birds feared to perch; in those coverts wild beasts would not lie down; no wind ever bore down upon that wood, nor thunderbolt hurled from black clouds; the trees, even when they spread their leaves to no breeze, rustled of themselves. Water, also, fell there in abundance from dark springs. The images of the gods grim and rude were uncouth blocks formed of felled tree-trunks. Their mere antiquity and the ghastly hue of the rotten timber struck terror...

Legend also told that often the subterranean hollows quaked and bellowed, that yew trees fell down and rose again, that the glare of conflagrations came from trees that were not on fire, and that serpents twined and glided round their stems. The people never resorted thither to worship at close quarters, but left the place to the gods. For, when the sun is in mid-heaven or dark night fills the sky, the priest himself dreads their approach and fears the lord of the grove.

(Pharsalia 3. 400-25)

The Roman historian Tacitus (c. 56 AD – c. 120 AD) later gave an account of the rout of the Druids on Anglesey in 59 AD, referring to *'groves sacred to savage rites'*, which were cut down: *'for their religion encouraged them to drench their altars with the blood of prisoners and to find out the will of the gods by consulting the entrails of human beings'.*

THE CELTS AND JULIUS CAESAR

There are few artefacts and no contemporary written sources to further illuminate the lives of our Stone Age and Bronze Age ancestors.

But of the Celtic peoples who arrived in Britain from around the seventh century BC, bringing with them the technology for iron-smelting, more is known to us. The meagre archaeological evidence is from this point supplemented by the writings of the Greeks and the Romans, whose territorial ambitions the Celts often came into conflict with during their own migrations from central Europe.

Contemporary Roman sources, such as those of the Emperor Julius Caesar, usually refer to the Celts as a race of war-loving barbarians – partly, no doubt, to justify their own 'civilising' ambitions in Europe. Caesar though, had a number of other reasons for his British invasion attempts in 55 and 54 BC (not least the control of the island's mineral wealth). Among them was a desire to destroy the influence wielded by the the Druids, the Celtic priesthood, whose power base, Caesar believed, lay in Southern Britain. The Belgic tribes who dwelt in both Britain and Gaul were amongst Rome's most stubborn opponents, and invasion of Britain began to look increasingly likely, when, having conquered Gaul in 58 BC, Caesar had reason to suspect the Druids in southern England of fuelling dissent amongst their Gaulish neighbours.

In the event, Caesar's British invasion attempts were only partially successful, and it would be ninety years before another military campaign was undertaken.

Perhaps a certain reluctance to return to this mysterious land beyond the ocean contributed to the delay. The Roman historian, Tacitus, was to write:

'Men coming from these remote regions, told strange stories – of hurricanes, unknown birds, sea monsters, and shapes half-human and half-animal.'

Julius Caesar's own description of the Britons' bizarre appearance in battle can have been no more encouraging: *'All the Britons dye their bodie's with woad, which produces a blue colour.... they wear their hair long and shave the whole of their bodies except the hair and upper lip.'*

THE CELTIC HERITAGE

Despite their oft-quoted love of warfare, the true legacy of the Celts has unquestionably been an artistic one, as evidenced in many exquisitely crafted objects, largely in metals, decorated in a distinctive free-flowing style. They had too, a strong oral tradition in poetry and music which flourished under the tutelage of the Druidic priesthood. These skills of story-telling kept alive, in cycles of epic narrative, tales of the gods and the deeds of long-dead ancestors.

The Celts had a profound reverence for sacred places in the natural world, and it seems likely that it was they who constructed a wooden causeway which led from the banks of the River Avon to the source of the Sacred Spring. Coins of the Dobunni, the Celtic tribe who lived in this part of North Somerset at the time of the Roman invasion, have been found in the spring, suggesting that these were votive offerings to the deity which they associated with the waters: Sulis.

Illustration of Bladud, by William Hoare.
From John Wood's *Essay towards a description of Bath*.
First published in 1742.

BLADUD'S TALE

The oral tradition of the Celts may well have been what kept the Legend of Prince Bladud alive long enough to be written down by the twelfth-century Welsh chronicler, Geoffrey of Monmouth in his *History of the Kings of Britain*. The book, a curious mixture of history, myth and folklore, was written in an age of sovereign enthusiasm for tracing lineage to the great kings of the past: one Saxon king claimed ancestry dating back to Caesar, another, back to the biblical Adam!

The tale of Bladud and his discovery of the hot springs of Bath in the fifth century BC, has undergone countless revisions and embellishments throughout the many hundreds of years of its existence. This is the basic story with one or two of its later adornments:

The young Prince Bladud having contracted leprosy on his return journey from a period of study in Athens, was confined to a room within the palace of his father, King Hudibras, lest the disease should spread throughout the Royal Court. But the headstrong prince, wearying of his enforced quarantine, escaped and fled the kingdom, taking up employment as a lowly swineherd. But after a time, Bladud discovered that the pigs too had become infected.

So it was that one day he approached the River Avon, herding his pigs down to the bottom of a steep, wooded valley to forage for acorns. As he waited for the pigs to feed, he noticed a few of them wallowing in a steaming alder swamp not far from the river bank. He was amazed to see that when the pigs emerged from the muddy waters their sores had been healed. Bladud followed their example and found that he too had been healed of his leprosy. The prince was thus able to return to his father's court and the joyful welcome of his family.

Some versions of the story relate that Bladud was a master of druidical magic and that when he became king he built a fabulous palace and centre of healing close to the hot springs. His over-reaching ambition led him to devise a pair of mechanical wings which, failing him in mid-flight, plunged him to his death on Solsbury Hill. His son, Lear, would one day be immortalised in Shakespeare's play, *King Lear*.

The outflow from the Roman reservoir.
A quarter of a million gallons of water a day flow from the Sacred Spring, at a more or less constant temperature of 46C. The two smaller springs to the west; the Cross Bath and the Hot Bath springs, produce over 24,000 gallons a day, at temperatures of 40C and 49C respectively. Oxidised iron salts in the water cause the ochre discoloration.

THE ROMAN OCCUPATION OF BATH

Almost a century after Julius Caesar's inconclusive expeditions, the Romans completed the subjugation of the Celtic tribes of lowland Britain. The successful military campaign of 43 AD, under the command of Aulus Plautius, was followed by an occupation which would last for nearly four hundred years, and which would dramatically alter the Valley of the Sacred Spring.

Within the first year of their arrival, the Roman troops had secured a frontier zone along the Jurassic limestone ridge from Lyme Bay to the Humber Estuary and had begun construction of the great military linking highway, the Fosse Way, to speed the movement of troops and supplies to the new garrison towns. The Fosse Way crossed the River Avon close to the springs, and the area would almost certainly have been garrisoned for a time while the local populations were being subdued. Any Celtic holy site which existed in the vicinity of the springs would more than likely have been destroyed by the Roman commanders in order to break the power of the local Druids.

But the Romans did not have things all their own way in the first years of the occupation: troubles flared up in the north and east of the country, partly as a result of an ill-judged decision by the Roman administrators to build a massive classical temple in Colchester, deifying the Emperor Claudius (to whom the success of the invasion had been attributed). This act of provocation led to a local uprising under the leadership of the queen of the Iceni tribe, Boudicca, and to the widespread destruction of much of the Roman province. But once the rebellion had been ruthlessly suppressed by the superior tactical skills of the Roman army, a climate of conciliation prevailed, and a new respect for local traditions was encouraged by a generation of more politically astute Roman administrators.

The south-west of the country, which had escaped the worst of the violence, now found itself among the main beneficiaries of the newly enlightened regime. The reverence which both races would undoubtedly have held for the hot springs, offered a unique means of bridging the cultural differences betweeen them:

Sul, the Celtic goddess of the waters, and Minerva, the Roman goddess of wisdom and healing, were united to create a single deity: Sulis Minerva. This conflation of the two belief systems, with its single point of worship, was to be a powerful symbol of the co-existence of the Roman and Celtic cultures in Britain. This was achieved, as the Roman historian, Tacitus, later expressed it: *'In order that a race of rude and primitive men, versed in the arts of war, might be rendered peaceful and tranquil, through the delights of luxury.'*

Around the Sacred Spring the Romans developed a religious sanctuary and spa, dedicated to Sulis Minerva, which was to become famous throughout the Empire. The settlement which grew out of this unification would be called Aquae Sulis: the Waters of Sul.

The Roman Great Bath, built around 70 AD,
was the largest of a suite of baths fed by the Sacred Spring.

THE GREAT BATH

The construction of the Roman Baths began around 65 AD with
the taming of the great spring. First, the surrounding marshland
was drained and the spring enclosed within a watertight lead-lined
reservoir wall. Thus harnessed, the hot waters were channelled
into a suite of baths which formed the central attraction of an
immense leisure complex. The showcase was the Great Bath, once
enclosed in a massive stone vault with high clerestory windows.

THE SACRED SPRING

At some stage in its development the Sacred Spring was also roofed over. The effect was to create a far more mysterious atmosphere – much like stepping into a vast, steaming cavern, its walls suffused with a rippling greenish light.

Isolated from the hustle and bustle of the bathing establishment crowd, the spring would have retrieved its primeval quietude, broken only by the echoes of the bubbling waters and the hushed voices of pilgrims come to seek an audience with the goddess Sulis Minerva.

Excavations of the spring in recent years have revealed a wealth of objects cast into the spring as votive offerings including coins, carved gemstones, brooches, bracelets and ivory. More fascinating, for what they reveal about everyday life in Roman Bath, are small scrolls of pewter and lead on which were inscribed messages to the goddess, many of them asking her to avenge some grievance or to intercede in a family dispute. One example is a small lead plaque 4 inches square upon which a curse has been scratched backwards so that only the goddess would understand it: *'May he who carried off Vilbia from me become as liquid*

as the water, May she who so obscenely devoured her become dumb, whether Velvinna, Exsupereus, Severinus, Augustalia, Comitianus, Catusminianus, Germanilla or Jovina.'
Another, less tantalisingly obscure inscription reads:

Dodimedis has lost two gloves. He asks that the person who has stolen them should lose his mind and his eyes in the temple where she appoints.

THE ROMAN BATHS

Today, in the hushed reverence with which one approaches the
2000-year-old remains of the Roman Baths, it is not easy to
imagine what a noisy, exuberant place the Roman bathing
establishment would have been: the richly frescoed walls of the
Great Bath echoing to the sounds of diving and splashing; the
slapping and pummelling of masseurs at work in the adjacent
massage rooms; the puffing and grunting of weight-lifters showing
off their physical form and prowess in exercise rooms; the
exhilarated cries of patrons emerging from the intense heat of the
sauna into the cold plunge bath. In corridors and passageways,
there would have been joke-telling and laughter; the hushed tones
of some slanderous gossip shared; perhaps the occasional groan of
an ageing legionary slowly immersing himself in the warm bath in
the hope of easing the discomfort of rheumatism (no doubt
worsened by the long British winters). There were quieter rooms
too, for the conducting of business transactions and playing board
games, and rooms for the essential rituals of daily bathing which
were such a vital part of the Roman way of life.

THE TEMPLE OF SULIS MINERVA

To the north of the sacred spring the Romans developed the
spiritual centre of Aquae Sulis, a vast religious sanctuary
dominated by a classical temple dedicated to the goddess Sulis
Minerva. Approached from the east along a paved avenue ending in
a flight of steps, the temple was raised high on a limestone
podium, its east-facing façade a richly carved pediment decorated
with symbols of the presiding deities supported on four Corinthian
columns.

Within the temple burned an eternal flame attended by priests,
which Solinus, writing in the third century AD, mentions in a
collection of pieces describing unusual phenomena of the Roman
Empire: *'Furnished luxuriously for human use...over these springs
Minerva presides and in her temple the perpetual fire never whitens
to ash, but as the flame fades, turns to rocky lumps.'*

The 'rocky lumps' that Solinus refers to, are most probably the
cinders of Somerset coal, of which there were accessible outcrops
close to the Fosse Way.

The paved and colonnaded courtyard surrounding the temple
contained many other religious and ceremonial buildings
commemorating a pantheon of gods. Below the temple stood a
sacrificial altar bearing carvings of traditional Roman gods such as
Bacchus, Jupiter and Apollo, at either side of which were shrines
dedicated to Sol, god of the sun, and to Luna, the moon goddess.

Further east, beyond the entrance to the sanctuary, stood a
circular temple, or Tholos – possibly on the site which the present
day abbey occupies.

THE STATUE OF THE GODDESS MINERVA

The life-sized gilded bronze head of Minerva was discovered in 1727 by workmen digging a sewer trench in Stall Street. The statue, complete with a high Corinthian helmet may well have stood inside the Roman Temple of Sulis Minerva. The remains of most of the Temple now lie up to fifteen feet below the present level of the city, in an area west of the current Pump Rooms.

THE 'GORGON'S' HEAD FROM THE TEMPLE PEDIMENT

The most fascinating detail of the Temple pediment is without doubt the so-called 'Gorgon's Head' centrepiece. The Gorgon, a symbol associated with the Minerva cult, was usually female, but this figure is most definitely male, and displays the muscular, free-flowing style of Celtic, not Roman, artistry. It may itself be a conflation of the Classical Gorgon and the Celtic Sul, merged into the guise of a sun god.

Despite a fierce intensity, the eyes of the Gorgon are almost quizzical – a distinct contrast to the finely sculpted but expressionless gaze of the Minerva statue.

The shield bearing this figure is bordered by oak wreaths – an important symbolic inclusion for both cultures – perhaps acknowledging the Druidic tradition in the region.

ROMAN CEREMONIAL MASK

Larger than life-size mask of tin, which had once been
attached to a wooden backing. The wood prevented the
mask from sinking to the bottom of the reservoir.

AQUAE SULIS

Around the nucleus of the Baths and the Temple Complex, developed a small but thriving urban settlement: a commercial area of shops and stalls, lodging houses and entertainments, all serving the needs of a regular influx of visitors from all over the Roman Empire.

The town was supported by a flourishing agricultural community, making it an important market centre for the surrounding area. Local industries such as pewter manufacturing and stone-masonry helped sustain a suburban population mainly spread along the river and the lower northern slopes. But it was Aquae Sulis' reputation as both spiritual retreat and leisure resort which was central to its importance in Roman times; dual roles which would define the town right down to the present day. (Although worldly pleasure and religious devotion would not always dwell together in such apparent harmony.)

Life would have been good in the town during those times when the Roman occupation was at its most stable. For a foot-weary legionary, perhaps on leave from campaigns in one of the troubled areas of the province, it must have been a re-assuring sight: those first glimpses of the town nestled in the river valley, protected by its seven hills and with its familiar Mediterranean-style white-stone buildings and red-tiled roofs. Here was a place to forget troubles for a while; perhaps to indulge in the occasional siesta (encouraged by the unusually enervating climate) and to enjoy the thermal waters, the theatre and the many other sensual diversions the town had to offer. In the Temple Sanctuary, homage would be paid to the gods, and time for quiet reflection be found, to gather strength and courage before picking up the legion's banner once more.

But the relative peace and stability which Romans and Britons enjoyed in this far-flung corner of the Empire could not last forever. Towards the end of the occupation a defensive wall was built around Aquae Sulis, perhaps as a response to the increased number of raids the country as a whole was suffering, from Saxons and other land-hungry peoples from across the North Sea.

The Roman Empire was under pressure on all of its borders, and by the beginning of the fifth century the central administration in Rome had collapsed. In an attempt to shore up defences at its heart, the army was recalled from the fringes of the Empire, and Britons were left to cope with successive waves of foreign invasion as best they could.

MOSAIC FLOOR

On the outskirts of the walled settlement and beyond, a number of high-status Roman style villas were built. To date over thirty sites have been discovered and there are almost certainly more buried beneath the foundations of present buildings. The sea-beasts mosaic, featuring dolphins and sea horses, was found during excavations in what was once the north-east corner of the walled settlement.

THE POST-ROMAN TWILIGHT WORLD

When the Romans deserted Aquae Sulis, early in the fifth century, they left behind an essentially Celtic tribal society ill-equipped, and perhaps unwilling, to sustain the sophisticated urban infrastructure that had been provided and maintained for almost four centuries. The Celtic-Romano population fled back to the old tribal hill-sites, abandoning the town altogether. As law and order broke down, inter-tribal enmities re-emerged. Large numbers of the Dobunni tribe migrated to mainland Europe sometime in the sixth century, leaving much of the local farmland to fall out of use. Many of the skills necessary for maintaining the urban settlement, such as glass-making, were lost or forgotten. (Window glass would not be made again for many centuries.) Gradually streets reverted to rubble and grasses, and the once thriving spa became little more than a ghost town.

The Baths were the first to suffer neglect. In fact they may have fallen into disuse long before the last Roman legionary had fled these shores. Rising sea levels in the fourth century had caused the low-lying areas of the settlement, which included the Bathing complex, to be periodically flooded by the River Avon. The flood waters backed up along drains and outfalls, leaving behind each time, layers of mud and silt, which had to be removed before the Baths could be used again. Once the hydraulic engineers who had carried out this essential maintenance had gone, there was probably no-one sufficiently skilled among the native population to undertake the necessary repairs.

Once the roofs had fallen in, it was only a matter of time before the general decay was hastened; each successive fall of masonry being buried by mud left behind by the worsening floods. In time the area around the spring returned to marsh, although the remains of the Temple and Baths stood for at least another four centuries at the centre of a rubble-strewn and sulphurous pool. It must have been a forlorn, yet still strangely impressive sight.

Locally quarried stone found a further use from around the middle of the third century when inhumation replaced cremation in funeral ceremonies.

Many gravestones have been discovered in different sites outside the walled settlement.

This one reads:

Lucius Vitellius Tancinus, son of Mantaius, a tribesman of Caurium in Spain, trooper of the cavalry regiment of Vettones. Roman citizen, aged 46, of 26 years service lies buried here.

A SAXON REFLECTION ON THE ROMAN CITY

This poem, written sometime in the eighth century, poignantly describes the crumbling city of Aquae Sulis:

THE RUIN

Wondrous is this masonry, shattered by the Fates. The city has been broken, and the fortifications raised by giants are crumbling. The roofs have fallen and the towers are in ruins. Fissures rent these roofless towers, and there is rime on the mortar. The battlements are mutilated and fallen to ruin, undermined by age. The master builders are perished and gone, held in the earth's embrace by the ruthless grip of the grave, whilst a hundred generations of mankind have passed away....Glorious were the many palatial buildings of the city, its baths and high towered gables. Many were the banqueting halls full of mirth until all was shattered by obdurate fate. The dead lay scattered on all sides. Pestilence came and all the warriors were carried off by death. Their fortresses became waste places, and the city decayed, and those who should have repaired them lay dead on the earth. Henceforth those dwellings crumbled away and large red tiles that shade the rafters of the roofs have fallen, cracked and broken among the ruins, where many a mailed warrior, merry and adorned in radiant gold, proud and flushed with wine, had looked on treasures of silver and precious stones, on untold wealth of gems, in this rich, spacious and magnificent city.

The Ruin is an extract from a collection of writings called the Exeter Book, given by Leofric, the first Bishop of Exeter, to the Cathedral library in 1072.

In an age where the skills of reading and writing were the preserve of a privileged few, it is likely that *The Ruin* was written by a monk, perhaps living and working in the nearby monastery, or on a pilgrimage to the sacred sites of England.

SAXON BATH

St Adhelm's Cross, said to be part of an eighth century Wessex cross, set up in 709 AD, to mark one of the nightly resting places of Adhelm, classical scholar-monk and Abbot of Malmesbury, as his body was being carried to Malmesbury for burial.

The years that followed the withdrawal of the Roman forces, were to be an unsettled age for the native Britons, as they struggled to either establish a new identity, or reassert a long neglected or forgotten one. The Saxon invaders soon began the long process of carving up the countryside into separate kingdoms, but it was many years before their presence was fully felt in the south-west, where there was fierce resistance from Romano-Celtic warrior chiefs such as King Arthur. A battle against a large Saxon army is reputed to have been fought and won by Arthur at Mount Badon around 520 AD. Badon, one of the names the Saxons later gave to Bath, may possibly refer to Lansdown, on the northern slopes of the town.

But virtually no documented evidence of these 'Dark Ages' has survived, and Bath effectively passes out of recorded history until the Anglo-Saxon Chronicle, written in the ninth Century, makes reference to the capture of the town in 57 AD by Saxon forces at the Battle of Dyrham. Bath now found itself on the borders of two great Saxon kingdoms: to the north, Mercia, to which Bath was ceded after its capture, and to the south, Wessex, which, in the ninth century, would supplant Mercia as the most powerful of the Saxon kingdoms.

Romano-Celtic Christians had worshipped in Britain since at least the time of the conversion of Emperor Constantine in 312 AD, although it is impossible to say how numerous they were. But with the coming of Augustine in the early years of the seventh century, there began the missionary evangelising of the Saxon kings which would lead to Bath's re-emergence into the light of history.

In 675 AD the Mercian King, Osric, granted lands to Abbess Berta to build a convent for the order of the Holy Virgins, thus establishing, as far as we know, the long period of ecclesiastical history in the town. Exactly where the first monastic buildings were, is as yet unknown, though Saxon burials discovered close to the site of the Sacred Spring suggest they may have been within the Roman Temple Precinct. Augustine, who had passed through the city in 603 AD, had been instructed by Pope Gregory I to make use of pagan temples, but to destroy the images in them. It may well be that during the building of the Convent, the Roman Temple pediment, with its pagan symbols, was finally toppled and laid out face down in a Christian monastic precinct.

SAXON BATH

The next recorded evidence, a charter of 757 AD, granted further lands, to the brothers of a monastic church of St. Peter. At this time a church was built almost certainly on, or close to, the site of the present abbey. The completed church was described in a Charter of 957 AD as having been built *'with marvellous workmanship'* – the use of cut stone from the Roman Temple and Baths would undoubtedly have contributed to this impression.

By the ninth century, Bath was under the rule of the Wessex kings and Benedictine monks were in control of the Saxon monastery, itself at the heart of a major religious centre and prosperous wool town.

What use was made of the springs is not known, but that their reputation as a place of healing and pilgrimage was still recognised, is reflected in another of the Saxon names for the town: Akemanceaster, which has been variously interpreted, but more often as either *'The sick men's town'* or *'City of the waters'*. Hat Bathu is the Saxon name from which – slightly more straightforwardly – Bath is derived.

Little remains of Bath's Saxon heritage, but the street grid which was established within the city walls (two sections divided by an east-west street, each divided into four north-south aligned streets) can still, in part, be traced in the street plan today.

The victories of Alfred, King of Wessex, against Danish marauders in the ninth century, helped to pull the disparate Saxon kingdoms into a kind of unity and Bath was to play a leading role in this unification of the peoples of England: on the 11th May 973, in the Saxon Abbey, Edgar was crowned King of all England by Dunstan, Archbishop of Canterbury and Oswald, Archbishop of York. The ceremony was to provide the template for all future coronations in England.

The town's position on the borders of two great Saxon kingdoms made it the perfect choice for such an important occasion, and the ceremony, in a monastery of national repute, symbolised the close relationship between the Church and the Kings. Edgar, already king for fourteen years, had post-

Fragment of late-Saxon stone cross found close to the Sacred Spring. The carved interlaced patterns, display the artistic influence of the Celts.

poned his coronation until his thirtieth year, some say, in order to coincide with the age that he could be ordained to the priesthood.

Posterity has credited him with the title of 'Edgar the Peaceable', but his hopes of sustaining peace were not to be realised: within two years of his coronation he was dead, and the country was once again being threatened with invasion from across the North Sea.

The King Edgar Window in Bath Abbey, celebrates the coronation of King Edgar, first king of all England, in 973 AD.

JOHN DE VILLULA AND THE NORMAN MONASTERY

William the Conqueror's victory at the Battle of Hastings in 1066, brought a new ruling dynasty to power in the country and introduced a feudal system of social organisation which was to have a profound effect on the fabric of English society for centuries to come.

Although Bath was left comparatively unscathed in the early years of this transition, in 1087 King William I died and an unsuccessful rebellion against the succession of his son, William Rufus, led to the widespread destruction of much of the town, including its Saxon abbey.

The new king appointed his physician John de Villula as Bishop of Wells and, mindful of the fact that much of what he owned there had been destroyed anyway, granted him the abbey at Bath with all its land and properties.

An educated and ambitious man, John de Villula was quick to seize the potential opportunities that the religious centre and its curative springs presented. In 1091 he transferred the See of the Somerset bishopric from Wells to Bath and set about a large scale re-planning of the town. He immediately pulled down what remained of the Saxon abbey, and began an ambitious building programme which included a monastic complex that was to cover a quarter of the walled area of the town and, in so doing, destroy much of the Saxon street grid in the south-east of the city.

A new cathedral was planned, so vast that the present abbey would have taken up no more space than that occupied by its nave. When the Cathedral priory was completed, some 40 years after John de Villula's death in 1122, it was one of the largest churches in England. The cathedral itself, 90 feet wide and over 350 feet long, stood in a monastic complex containing chapter house, cloister, refectory, infirmary and Prior's lodging. The Bishop's Close in the south-west corner of the new complex contained the Bishop's Palace and one of the city's Saxon churches: St. James. (Although it was not long before it was partially demolished and appropriated for use as a private chapel for the bishop.) There were baths too, fed by the King's Bath Spring, for the exclusive use of the priors and abbots.

Architecturally, John de Villula transformed the nucleus of the city in no less a dramatic fashion than the Romans had done a thousand years before him and, in so doing, established a religious centre and seat of learning to rival Aquae Sulis.

THE GESTA STEPHANI

As a skilled physician John de Villula would have been well aware of the reputed healing properties of the hot springs, and it was most probably on his instruction that a new bath was constructed over the site of the surviving Roman reservoir for the use of royal guests. It is still known as The King's Bath to this day.

The earliest known reference to the healing qualities of the springs is contained in the *Gesta Stephani (the works of King Stephen)* dating from 1138 and of anonymous authorship: *'...a city where little springs, through hidden conduits, send up waters heated without human skills or ingenuity from deep in the bowels of the earth to a basin vaulted over with noble arches, creating in the middle of the town, baths of agreeable warmth...the sick are wont to gather there from all England to wash away their infirmities in the health giving waters, and the whole to see the wondrous jets of water and bathe in them.'*

ADELARD THE SCHOLAR MONK

The twelfth-century English historian and monk, William of Malmesbury, tells us that John de Villula: *'completed many things nobly in ornaments and books, and filled the abbey with monks eminent for literature and discharge of their duties.'*

The collegiate school which he established in Bath was attended by the eminent scholar monk, Adelard. Adelard travelled in Europe and the Middle East, learning Greek and Arabic philosophy, science and medicine, before settling in Bath around 1126 to write his famous treatise on the astrolabe. The twelfth century saw a tremendous diffusion of Greek, Latin and Arab influences throughout Europe, and with papal authority extending over the entire continent, monks – the great travellers of the time – were in a unique position to disseminate these influences. In this way the great religious houses became the repositories for the new, exciting knowledge being brought back from cultures with ancient traditions in the sciences and medicine. These may well have provided a new validity to the long established belief in the efficacy of the spring waters, and an aid in fulfilling the Benedictine monastic duties to the sick and the poor.

THE HOSPITAL OF ST JOHN THE BAPTIST

The two hot springs to the west of the monastic precinct, provided the setting for the first of the medieval almshouses to be built within the walled city. The Hospital of St John the Baptist was founded in 1174 by the Bishop of Bath, Reginald Fitz Josceline, and provided accommodation and access to the healing waters for eight of the local elderly poor, who, distinguished by their blue gowns, were known as the 'Blue Alms'.

The archway leading to **St Johns Hospital.** The hospital was rebuilt, in part, by John Wood the Elder in 1727, and still provides accommodation for the elderly, making it one of the longest surviving almshouses in the country.

The East Window of the chapel in St. John's Hospital, featuring Christ among the lilies. The chapel was designed by William Killigrew in 1717.

After much battling for prestige, Bath was to share cathedral status with Wells from 1245, but the Bishop's seat more or less permanently moved to Wells, which was soon to see the completion of its own impressive cathedral. Morale slumped dramatically in the Bath monastery, and the abbey buildings and baths entered a long period of neglect and decline.

The economy of the town as a whole, however, prospered, and the extensive estates owned by the abbey still provided the livelihoods of most of the town's inhabitants. The wool trade was central to this prosperity and both the monks and townspeople were involved in spinning, weaving and the sale of manufactured cloth – the Priory even owned its own fulling mill on the Avon (for the repair of which it was often accused of removing stones from the city wall). The presence locally of Fuller's Earth (used for cleaning fleeces) ensured that the entire process of manufacturing could be accomplished within the city. Spinners, fullers, weavers and dyers, together with merchants, labourers and servants, comprised the majority of occupations in the city.

That Bath in the Middle Ages was more renowned for its cloth trade than its healing springs, is acknowledged in one of Geoffrey Chaucer's *Canterbury Tales, 'The Wife of Bath'*. It is said of Dame Alison: *'Of clooth-making she hadde swiche an haunt, She passed hem of Ypres, and of Gaunt.'*

The Chapel of St Mary Magdalen,
rebuilt by Prior Cantlow around 1490.

THE HOSPITAL OF ST MARY MAGDALEN

South of the river, on the steep slopes of the Holloway, lay the
Hospital of St. Mary Magdalen. Originally an almshouse for poor
lepers – hence its position, well outside the city walls – it may well
have pre-dated the Hospital of St. John. In the later Middle Ages,
when leprosy was less prevalent, the site became a private chapel
for the priors of Bath.

In the grounds stands a Judas Tree. From one such tree Judas
Iscariot was said to have hanged himself. Each Lent it displays
purple blossoms, believed to represent 'tears of blood'.

THE HOLLOWAY

Opinions vary as to the origins of the name of this ancient trackway. Possible derivations include the 'haulway', a reference, presumably, to the practicalities of transporting goods by cart up the steep hill to Beechen Cliff, site of one of the city's medieval fairs. Another source suggests that the road, which lay on the pilgrimage route to Glastonbury, was once known as the 'Holy Way'. A more probable explanation is that it derives from the sunken-nature of the track which had been in use since prehistoric times and formed part of the route of the Roman Fosse Way. In the sixteenth century, however, it was a haven for the, by then, infamous beggars of Bath, who were able to take advantage of the fact that the area lay outside the jurisdiction of the city. The situation got so bad that two sixteenth-century Acts of Parliament designed to control vagrancy specifically mentioned Bath. Holloway retained its reputation for deprivation and poverty well into the twentieth century.

JOHN LELAND

The impact of Caxton's printing press and the influence of the European Renaissance, inspired a new passion for learning in the sixteenth century, and the ancient monastic libraries, hitherto largely inaccessible to the secular community, were sought out at last for the intellectual wealth they contained. It was down the steep track of the Holloway, in 1540, that John Leland came on his way to Bath, with a warrant from King Henry VIII, to search the collegiate libraries of England, so that the works of ancient writers *'Mighte be brought owte of deadely darkness to lyvely light'*. Leland, a schoolmaster and antiquarian, personified this new thirst for exploration and discovery: *'I was totally inflamed,'* he told Henry VIII, *'with a love to see thoroughly all those parts of your opulent and ample realm that I had read of...'*.

Or ever I cam to the bridge of Bath that is over Avon I cam doun by a rokky hille fulle of fair springes of water: and on this rokky hille is sette a longe streate as a suburbe to the cyte of Bath: and this streat is a chapelle of S. Mary Magdalen. Ther is a great gate with a stone arche at the entre of the bridge. The bridge hath v. fair stone arches. Bytwixt the bridge and the south gate of Bath I markid fair medows on eche hand, but especially on the lift hond, and they ly by south west on the toun. The cite of Bath is sette booth yn a fruteful and pleasant botom, the which is environid on every side with greate hilles, out of the which cum many springes of pure water that be conveyid by dyverse ways to serve the cite. Insomuch that leade beyng made ther at hand many houses yn the toune by the names of est, west, north and south.

From: *The Itinerary of John Leland.*

On a later journey to Bath, Leland wrote of weed-grown ruins in the abbey grounds. These were not the ruins of the Anglo-Saxon abbey, but of John de Villula's Norman cathedral: forty years before John Leland began his travels through England, the immense church had been destroyed leaving virtually no trace.

OLIVER'S ABBEY

At the close of the Middle Ages the monastery at Bath was still prosperous, but a succession of Royal charters had granted an increasing amount of power to the city authorities. The Black Death had devastated both secular and religious communities and by the end of the fifteenth century, the total number of monks in Bath had been halved to around twenty – in a monastery which dominated a quarter of the area within the city walls.

When Bishop Oliver King visited Bath in 1499, he found an abbey almost derelict, and a priory in which almsgiving was neglected. There was feasting in the refectory, and women were often to be seen at *'unseemly times'* in the monastery precinct. Determined to stop the rot,

the bishop took matters into his own hands. By reducing the income of the prior and monks and restricting allowances for food, drink, clothing, and estate management, he was able to save enough money to begin a complete restoration of the monastic establishment. This entailed the demolition of the ruined Norman Cathedral and the building of an abbey church on a more modest scale than its predecessor.

The inspiration behind Oliver King's timely intervention in the fate of the monastery at Bath, is said to have come from a vision, in which he saw the Holy Trinity and a host of angels ascending and descending a ladder from heaven, at the foot of which was an olive tree supporting a crown. In his dream a voice spoke to him, saying:

'Let an olive establish the crown and let a king restore the church'.

Taking this to be a play on words relating partly to himself and partly to the king, Henry VII, he concluded that he was being called upon to support the Tudor line of monarchs and to rebuild the abbey church at Bath.

The task of construction, and that of restoring discipline and morality to the monastic community, he left to his prior, William Birde, who carried on the work after King's death in 1503.

BATH ABBEY – THE WEST FRONT

Oliver King's vision is recorded in stone on the west front of
the Abbey: climbing the buttresses on either side of the West
Window are carved angels going to-and-fro between heaven
and earth. The pun on his name is depicted in the carving of
an olive tree encircled by a crown, topped with a bishop's
mitre. On either side of the large central oak door are statues
of the patron saints of the abbey: Saint Peter and Saint Paul.
Over the same door stands a statue of Henry VII.

The fan-vaulting in the **Bath Abbey** choir by the Vertue brothers.

Birde employed Henry VII's masons, William and Robert Vertue, to design the abbey. The Vertues were experts in fan-vaulting, and promised '...*ther shal be noone so goodely neither in England nor in France*'. Neither of the Vertues lived to see their claims justified; almost three centuries were to pass before the fan-vaulting was at last completed.

The Abbey at Bath, built in late Gothic perpendicular style, was the last great architectural achievement of Catholic England.

THE DISSOLUTION OF THE ABBEY

When Bishop Oliver King died in 1503, his will stipulated that: *'a dyner and repaste be made for the poor, and not for the rich, for my remuneration is not in the place I go from, but, as my hope is, in that place which I go to'*.

This reminder of the monastic duties to the poor would have done little to alter the general perception in the Medieval period, that the Catholic church had done little to help right the social injustices of the time. The loss of common lands, the Black Death, the decline of the weaving industry, the rise of the merchant and craft guilds and the growing influence of the Reformation all fuelled a growing desire to wrest control from what was seen as a dissolute and self-interested church. Some of this power had been achieved by the city authorities through Royal charters, but there were still more profound changes to come.

In the summer of 1535, Dr. Richard Layton, one of Thomas Cromwell's commissioners, visited Bath priory and sent the following report to his employer: *'Hit may please yor goodnes to understande that we have visited Bathe. Wheras we found the prior a right vertuose man and I suppose no better of his cote, a man simple and not of the greteste wit; his monkes worse than I have founde yet both in bugerie and adulterie, sum one of them haveying 10 women, some 8, and the reste so fewer. the house well repaired but foure hundreth poundes in dett.'* The days of the cathedral priory were no doubt numbered before this slanderous account of life within the monastery walls was received. (Though attempts made by the prior to bribe Thomas Cromwell – *'The Hammer of the Monks'* – were possibly not in their best interests.) Henry VIII already had the motive he needed, when, in that same year, he made the break with Rome and established the Protestant Church in England with himself as monarch at its head.

Four years later the Bath abbey and all its estates were confiscated by the Crown – or that is to say all the estates that the monks still owned. On the eve of the Dissolution they had sold, or granted out on long-term leases, much of the land belonging to the priory to members of the local gentry, thus raising money for their own future needs. The commissioners, on seeking the formal surrender of the priory, were unwilling to arouse the hostility of the powerful beneficiaries of this arrangement and had no alternative but to honour the agreements. In so doing, the monks, who also received generous pensions as a result of their dismissals, emerged from the biggest shake-up in English ecclesiastical history having sustained their economic ties within the city.

Building work on the Abbey had not even been completed when, in 1539, it was offered to the citizens of Bath for 500 marks. Perhaps suspicious of a catch, or believing that the four parish churches already in the town were enough expense in maintaining, they turned down the offer. The abbey was instead stripped of anything valuable, including its lead, glass and bells and allowed to fall into ruin. After passing to a number of different owners, it was handed back to its citizens in 1572 – by which time it was little more than a shell.

THE ELIZABETH WINDOW

Ironically, it fell to Henry VIII's eldest child, the Protestant
Elizabeth I, to revive the fortunes of the abbey church, when, in
1574, the new queen visited Bath and gave her support to the
launching of a national appeal to roof the choir.

This window celebrates the restoration of the abbey by the citizens
of Bath, and commemorates Queen Elizabeth's contribution to the
task which was completed in 1616.

WILLIAM SHAKESPEARE AND BATH

In the artistic revival of the Elizabethan Era, bands of strolling minstrels and actors took to performing in the streets for money. In an effort to control the ever-growing numbers of them descending on provincial towns, a statute was passed forbidding illegal busking, the penalty for which was *'to be stripped naked from the middle upwards, and be openly whipped till his or her bodie be bloudie'*. Although it is unlikely that Shakespeare suffered this fate, it is thought that he performed in Bath, possibly with The Queen's Players, between 1587 and 1601. His visits to Bath, judging by the sonnets he wrote containing references to the town, owe more to a search for relief from venereal disease, which was rampant in the Elizabethan Era:

SONNET 153
> *Cupid laid by his brand and fell asleep,*
> *A maid of Dian's this advantage found,*
> *And his love-kindling fire did quickly steep*
> *In a cold valley-fountain of that ground,*
> *Which borrow'd from this holy fire of love*
> *A dateless lively heat, still to endure,*
> *And grew a seething bath, which yet men prove*
> *Against strange maladies a sovereign cure.*
> *But at my mistress' eye Love's brand new-fir'd*
> *The boy for trial needs would touch my breast;*
> *I, sick withal, the help of Bath desir'd,*
> *And thither hied, a sad distemper'd guest,*
> > *But found no cure; the bath for my help lies*
> > *Where Cupid got new fire – my mistress' eyes.*

SONNET 154
> *The little love-god lying once asleep*
> *Laid by his side his heart inflaming brand,*
> *Whilst many nymphs that vow'd chaste life to keep*
> *Came tripping by; but in her maiden hand*
> *The fairest votary took up that fire,*
> *Which many legions of true hearts had warm'd;*
> *And so the general of hot desire*
> *Was sleeping by a virgin hand disarm'd.*
> *This brand she quenched in a cool well by,*
> *Which from Love's fire took heat perpetual,*
> *Growing a bath, and healthful remedy*
> *For men diseas'd; but I, my mistress' thrall,*
> > *Came there for cure, and this by that I prove:*
> > *Love's fire heats water, water cools not love.*

BATH AFTER THE DISSOLUTION

The stripping of ecclesiastical power in the sixteenth century was to have a tremendous impact on English society: economic progress replaced religious influence as the major force of social change. It led to a period of great social unrest in which the church could do little for the needy and the sick. Epidemics, famines and loss of livelihood still brought increasing numbers of them to Bath in search of relief. But the chantry priests and almoners were gone, and the city authorities struggled to find solutions. As late as 1622, with the wool industry in its final decline, the mayor complained that: 'We are a verie little poore Citie, our clothmen much decayed and many of their workmene amongst us relieved by the Citie.'

A new source of revenue was urgently needed, and marketing the healing properties of the spa waters to the wealthy nobility seemed an obvious solution. After the dissolution, the hot baths had been removed from the jurisdiction of the Abbey, and a charter in the time of Queen Elizabeth I made the 'body of citizens, and their successors, perpetual guardians of the city and hot waters'. And so it was that the springs once again became central to the fortunes of the local economy.

In 1572 an Act of Parliament attempted to restrict the number of poor and diseased entering the city, and the early seventeenth century saw a further hardening of attitudes, with sometimes brutal sanctions against begging and other forms of, what were deemed to be, social misconduct. In time, less harsh compromises were reached, but it was a conflict which would haunt the City for many years to come.

Queen Elizabeth was to provide one more invaluable service to the spa: the Catholic tradition of seeking 'miracle cures' had been looked on with suspicion by Henry VIII, who had tried to suppress the use of holy springs for healing purposes. Catholics, however, had merely resorted to continental spas, thus sparking a fear that the seditious amongst them might assist in an invasion from the Spanish Netherlands. In order to prevent such an occurrence, secular promotion of English spas was encouraged during Elizabeth's reign.

Their use was further assisted by a spate of writings in the late sixteenth century, praising the healing properties of the waters. The first of these, published in 1562, was the 'Treatise on the Bath Waters' by the 'master of English Physicke', Dr William Turner. In 1572 John Jones 'Gent., Graduate in Physicke', wrote: 'The Bathes of Bathe Ayde, wonderful and most excellent, agaynst very many sicknesses, approved by authorities, confirmed by reason, and dayly tried by experience.'

THE BATHS IN THE SIXTEENTH AND SEVENTEENTH CENTURIES

Contemporary impressions of the baths in the sixteenth and seventeenth centuries suggest that the City had some trouble segregating the wealthy, who came to Bath seeking 'the cure', from the sick poor, who still flocked to the town in search of relief. The local population, judging by Thomas Johnson's vivid portrayal of the King's Bath, considered bathing more of a spectator event.

A vivid description of the difficulties the City seems to have had maintaining order in the baths is provided by the wording of a statute passed in 1646:

That no Man or Woman should go into any one of the Baths, by day or night, without Covering on their Bodies, under the Penalty of Three Shillings and Four Pence. That no Person shall presume to cast or throw any Dog, Bitch or other live beast into any of the said Baths, under the Penalty of Three Shillings and Four Pence. That no Person shall thrust, cast or throw another into any of the said Baths with his or her Clothes on, under Penalty of Six Shillings and Eight Pence...

Queen Anne of Denmark, the wife of James I, who visited the King's Bath in 1616, was fortunate enough (as far as we know) not to have any live animals hurled in her direction, but nevertheless did receive a shock which made her vow she would never use the bath again. She was alarmed whilst bathing, when, from the bottom of the cistern, a flame rose to the surface and spread out in a large circle of light over the water. Physicians tried to reassure her that it was merely 'marsh gas' and of natural origin – but she could not be consoled. Fortunately a newly built bath lay adjacent to the King's Bath and the Queen was persuaded to use it. The New Bath was henceforth renamed the 'Queen's Bath'.

As its reputation grew, the major occupations in the town changed from weaving to the keeping of lodging houses – many of them by members of the medical profession, who were soon said to outnumber patients. The changes which were creating a health resort for the wealthy were lamented by some. Daniel Defoe, for instance, in his *'Tour through the whole of the British Isles'*, wrote:

...in former times this was a resort for cripples, and we see the crutches hang up at the several baths, as the thank offerings of those who have come hither lame, and gone away cured. But now we may say it is the resort of the sound, rather than the sick, the bathing is made more of a sport and a diversion, than a physical prescription for health, and the town is taken up in raffling, gaming, visiting, and in a word, all sorts of gallantry and levity.

THE KING'S BATH

Thomas Johnston's drawing of 1675, depicts the King's Bath and the smaller Queen's Bath. In the centre is a structure known as the 'kitchen'. The changing facilities were primitive, consisting of a dank passageway where men and women undressed together.

THE BATHS IN THE SIXTEENTH AND SEVENTEENTH CENTURIES

John Leland, writing of his visit to the city in 1536, described the Cross Bath as:

much frequentid of people with Lepre, Pokkes, Scabbes and great Aches...the colour of the water is as it were a depe blewe sea water, and reeketh like a seething Pot continually, having sumwhat a sulphurous and sumwhat an onpleasant savour.

But by the end of the sixteenth century, the Cross Bath had become the most frequented by the 'quality', and for those seeking pleasure rather than treatment. Celia Fiennes, who first visited the city around 1687, wrote of her observations of Bath in *Through England on a side-saddle in the time of William and Mary.* She described the formal procedures for bathing:

The visitor was helped into bathing clothes by an attendant; canvas drawers and waistcoats for the men, and a capacious dress for women, with sleeves like a parson's gown...this was quickly filled up with water, thus disguising the shape. Guides, their skins tanned by constant immersion in the hot mineral waters, steered the bathers and held them upright until they found their balance. Ladies received from an attendant a little floating dish like a basin, into which the lady puts an handkerchief, a snuff-box and a nosegay.

Celia Fiennes also noted that there was now:

a serjeant belonging to baths that all the bathing tyme walks in galleryes and takes notice order is observed and punishes the rude.

But attempts to segregate the sexes do not appear to have been entirely successful, as Edward Ward observed in his satirical essay *'A step to the Bath'*, published in 1700. In this piece he describes some not altogether decorous behaviour at the Cross Bath:

Here is perform'd all the Wanton Dalliance imaginable; Celebrated Beauties, Panting Breasts, and Curious Shapes, almost expos'd to Public View; Languishing Eyes, Darting Glances, Tempting Amorous Postures, attended by soft Musick enough to provoke a Vestal to forbidden Pleasures... Here were also different Sexes, from Quality to Honourable Knights, Country Puts and City Madams.

THE CROSS BATH

One of the many claims made on behalf of the medical virtues of the waters was that they were able to cure, as Dr William Turner called it: *'Barunnes of man or woman'*. Mary of Modena, the childless wife of James II, visited the Cross Bath in 1687 in the hopes of producing an heir to the throne. She did in fact conceive not long after her visit, and a new cross of sculptured white marble was erected at the bath to commemorate the event and the proven efficacy of the spring waters. James II's hopes of keeping the Stuart line on the throne of England, however, were less successful. Soon both he and his new son would be in exile, and the Hanoverian line of King Georges would sit on the throne of England throughout most of the eighteenth century.

THE CROSS BATH

Along the walls of the Cross Bath, were hooks from which hung the crutches of people who claimed to have been cured of their sickness.

JOHN SPEED'S MAP OF BATH 1610

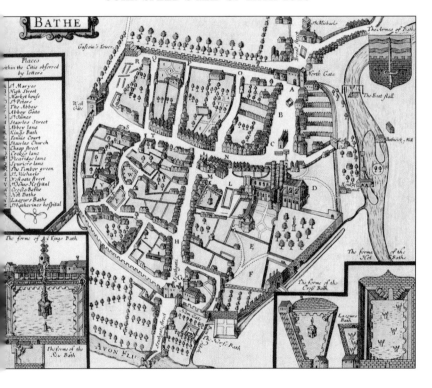

JOHN SPEED'S MAP OF BATH 1610

One of the earliest illustrations of the walled city of Bath was by the historian John Speed. The Saxon street plan is still clearly visible in the map, particularly north of the east-west axis of Westgate Street and Cheap Street. The High Street (one of those four north-south lanes still in existence in 1610) had been widened to accommodate the market which was held at the south end of the street. In 1625 the Market Hall was to be the site of a new Guildhall and Market.

The southern half of the city had witnessed dramatic alterations in Norman times – particularly in the south-east street plan, much of which was demolished to make way for John de Villula's cathedral complex and Bishop's Palace. A new central thoroughfare, Stall Street, was created, leading to the South Gate and the St. Lawrence Bridge.

The medieval gates of the city are visible on the map, including the East Gate leading to the Monks' Mill on the banks of the Avon. The East gate is the only one of the medieval gates to have survived to the present day. Also to be seen on the river, in the area known as The Boat Stall, is the rope-guided ferry – the only means of crossing the river to the east of the city once the weir (necessary for providing power to the wool mills) had been created.

Separate illustrations of the baths themselves are featured on the map, including the Lazars (Lepers) Bath. The Lepers Bath was demolished by John Wood in 1776, who described it as *'being the place of resource for the most miserable objects that seek relief from the healing fountains...it is proportionately mean, obscure and small'.*

BATH ON THE EVE OF THE GEORGIAN ERA

At the end of the seventeenth century, the city of
Bath, still confined within its medieval walls,
consisted of perhaps 250 houses and a population of
just over 1000.

Contemporary sources suggest that the town was
not a particularly pleasant place to live: when Queen
Elizabeth visited in 1574 she noted, with some
displeasure, that the main thoroughfare, Cheap
Street, was only seven feet wide and had an open
sewer running down the middle of it.

One hundred years later rubbish was still being
thrown into the streets and over the city wall. The
low-lying position of the town surely made this
practice even more unsavoury, prompting a visiting
Frenchman in the fourteenth century to advise: *'Bath,
situated, or rather buried, in deep valleys in the
middle of a thick atmosphere and a sulphureous fog, is
at the gates of Hell'.*

Although a 'scavenger' had been appointed in 1613
to remove household rubbish, the diarist John
Evelyn, who visited the city in 1654, could still
describe the streets as *'uneven, narrow and
unpleasant.'*

The architect John Wood, writing in the middle of
the eighteenth century, paints a far more graphic
picture of the state of the town:

*'The streets and public ways of the city were
become like so many dunghills, slaughter houses, pig
styes: for soil of all sorts, and even carrion, were cast
and laid in the streets, and the pigs turned out by day
to feed and rout among it; butchers killed and dressed
their cattle at their own doors; people washed every
kind of thing they had to make clean at the common
conduits in the open streets; and nothing was more
common than small racks and mangers at almost
every door for the baiting of horses.'*

51

SAMUEL PEPYS

Unlike John Evelyn, that other famous diarist of the seventeenth century, Samuel Pepys, was quite complimentary about the city. The diaries which he kept during a nine-year period of his life were written in code (probably with half a mind to keeping his numerous amorous assignations a secret from his wife).

Since being translated in the nineteenth century, they have provided an invaluable source of historical record for this period of English history which included the Great Fire of London. Pepys discontinued his diary in 1669, mistakenly believing his eyesight to be failing. Here are a few extracts from entries he made during a visit to Bath:

12th June. Friday.
...we came before night to the Bath; where I presently stepped out with my landlord, and saw the baths, with people in them. They are not so large as I expected, but yet pleasant; and the town most of stone, and clean, though the streets generally narrow. I home, and being weary, went to bed without supper, the rest supping.

13th June. Saturday.
Up at 4 a'clock being by appointment called up to the Cross Bath where we were carried after one another, myself, and wife and Betty Turner, Willett, and W.H. And by and by though we designed to have done before company came; very fine ladies; and the manner pretty enough, only methinks it cannot be clean to go with so many bodies together in to same water. Good conversation among them that are acquainted here, and stay together. Strange to see how hot the water is; and in some places, though this is the most temperate bath, the springs so hot as the feet not able to endure. But strange to see when women and men herein, that live all the season in these waters, that cannot but be parboiled, and look like the creatures of the Bath. Carried back, wrapped in a sheet, and in a chair, home; and there one after another thus carried (I staying above two hours in the water), home to bed, sweating for an hour; and by and by, comes music to play to me, extraordinary good as ever I heard at London almost, or anywhere.

SAMUEL PEPYS

14th June. Sunday.

Up, and walked up and down the town, and saw a pretty good market place, and many good streets, and very fair stone houses. And so to the great church, and there saw Bp. Montagu's tomb; and, when placed, did there see many brave people come, and, among other, two men brought in, in litters, and set down in the chancel to hear: but I did not know one face. Here a good Organ; but a vain, pragmatic fellow preached a ridiculous affected sermon, that made me angry, and some gent that sat next me and sang well. So home, walking round the walls of the city, which are good, and the battlements all whole.

Part of the medieval north wall of Bath still exists: with its *'battlements whole'* – as Pepys recorded in his diary.

BATH AND THE AGE OF ELEGANCE

The turbulent seventeenth century in England, which had seen civil war, the execution of King Charles I, the unpopular reign of a Puritan 'Lord Protector', Oliver Cromwell and the eventual restoration of the monarchy, looked as though it might end in further turmoil at the succession of the Catholic James II. But the final break with the Stuart line of monarchs came in 1688 with the 'Glorious Revolution', and a Bill of Rights which claimed the ascendancy of parliamentary power over sovereign rule. 'Personal liberty' was declared the 'inalienable right of every Englishman'.

In this bloodless revolution, James II was replaced by his Protestant daughter Mary and her husband William of Orange. The reforming Whig party, identified with the increasingly powerful commercial classes, looked forward to an unbroken spell in power lasting from 1714 to 1760. An era of new freedoms and opportunities beckoned, which was to confirm Bath's reputation as a resort of fashion and frivolity.

A succession of Royal visits, culminating in those of the popular Queen Anne in 1702 and 1703, were to prove most advantageous to the city's fortunes in the eighteenth century, for in the wake of these visits the aristocracy were to follow in hitherto unprecedented numbers.

The City, although it had courted this interest, found itself totally unprepared for the sudden influx of wealthy patrons, having still no decent lodgings, no suitable facilities for public assembly, and no entertainments other than a few pleasant walks and a bowling green.

The playwright, Oliver Goldsmith, described the pleasures afforded by spa towns such as the pre-Georgian Bath as *'merely rural; the company splenetic, rustic and vulgar'*. Riven with social problems which no amount of municipal legislation seemed wholly able to control, the City, in the face of these difficulties, might well have let the moment pass, and allowed Bath to slip back into its provincial torpor.

The city was saved from this probable outcome by the efforts of three quite different characters: Richard Nash, Ralph Allen, and John Wood. Self-made men, in an age where it was still not easy to rise above humble beginnings, between them they would transform, architecturally and culturally, a medieval backwater into one of the most beautiful and fashionable cities in Europe.

An unlikely aid to this transformation was a craze for gambling which had first swept England in the reign of Charles II. The aristocracy were looking for somewhere outside London where, as Oliver Goldsmith put it, *'They might have each other's company, and win each other's money as they had done during the winter in town'.* And so Bath became the focus of social life outside London – the 'Bath Season'.

It was this craze for gambling that brought to Bath the first of the 'Founding Fathers', Richard 'Beau' Nash – as unlikely a catalyst for the 'Age of Elegance' as gambling itself was.

RICHARD 'BEAU' NASH: THE 'KING OF BATH'
(1674-1761)

When Richard Nash arrived in Bath in 1705 it was with little more ambition, it seems, than to make a living from the gaming tables. At the age of thirty he had so far failed to complete a university course, or sustain careers in either the army or the law. Bath, with its rich and aristocratic summer visitors, keen to flaunt their wealth in each other's company, probably offered as good an opportunity as he was likely to get of improving his fortunes.

Much of what is known of the character of the 'King of Bath' we owe to the biography written by author and playwright Oliver Goldsmith: *A life of Richard Nash, Esq.*, in which the 'Beau' is portrayed as a likeable, humorous, essentially kind-hearted, yet slightly ridiculous man. The flamboyant dress sense which earned him his nickname, was somewhat out of keeping with the more sober style of the age and made more idiosyncratic by his habit of combining fashions of different periods to suit his personality. His sartorial trademark, a white beaver hat, was worn, he insisted, only to keep it from being stolen.

Gambling prowess, a dandyish appearance and a reputation for light-hearted buffoonery, could not perhaps be considered essential qualities for greatness, and were unlikely on their own to find him a place in the history of Bath. But Nash possessed certain other qualities which, combined with his exuberant personality, were to prove indispensable to the city, and ensure his contribution to the cultural and social development of the nation as a whole. Not the least of these qualities was an unparalleled flair for making things happen.

It was not long before he made his mark. In 1706 he became 'official' Master of Ceremonies after the previous incumbent, a Captain Webster, was killed in a sword fighting duel – a not uncommon hazard, particularly amongst gamblers – and a route which Nash was determined not to follow. One of the first rules he laid down was to ban duelling and the wearing of swords in public places. (But not, apparently, before having to fight a duel himself in order to prove that he was not merely imposing the rule as an act of cowardice on his part.) He rightly deduced that if Bath was to attract more of the wealthy nobility, regular brawling in the streets was probably not the best advertisement.

The new Bath Society was not governed by the strict rules which kept the nobility aloof from their social inferiors in London: for modest subscriptions rich merchants and country squires could rub shoulders with the aristocracy at the social occasions – a situation not much to the liking of those from the world of rank and fashion, and one which led to confrontation and fracas.

RICHARD 'BEAU' NASH: THE 'KING OF BATH'
(1674-1761)

Nash determined to root out this snobbery based on birth, putting a ban on all forms of private entertainment. Thus he set about dispelling the *'tincture of Gothic haughtiness'* which had kept the nobility and gentry segregated.

He imposed strict standards of etiquette and courtly manners, and equally strict standards of dress and behaviour at social occasions. His word was generally obeyed without question, whether by noble, gentry or peasant. Within a few short years of his arrival in Bath, all visitors to the city were bound to the codes of conduct which he laid down.

Nash next set about upgrading the social amenities of the town. He insisted that lodging houses were improved and that streets were paved, lighted, and cleaned regularly, and saw to it that the businesses of Sedan chairmen were properly regulated. (They had been known to abandon people in the rain if their inflated prices were not paid!) He raised the quality of entertainments, engaging professional musicians to play in the public places and, in 1706, collaborated in the opening of the first Assembly Rooms – soon to become the social hub of the city.

This civilising of Bath, which Richard Nash appears to have almost single-handedly achieved, was to create the wealth which would open the next chapter in its development. But Nash himself was not long to share the wealth he had done so much to establish: anti-gambling legislation in 1738-39 and 1745 dealt a severe blow to his fortunes from which he never fully recovered. Although he lived to be 87, much of his later life was spent in relative poverty and he became, to many, an object of ridicule. Oliver Goldsmith said of Nash: *'He had too much merit not to become remarkable and too much folly to arrive at greatness.'* and that *'he rose to the very summit of second class luxury'.* But in its closing pages, Goldsmith describes the qualities which may have contributed to the many affectionate outpourings that followed his death:

He could not stifle the natural impulse which he had to do good, but frequently borrow'd money to relieve the distressed; and when he knew not conveniently where to borrow, he has been often observed to shed tears, as he passed through the wretched supplicants who attended his gate. This sensibility, this power of feeling for the misfortunes of the miserable, and his address and earnestness in relieving their wants, exalts the character of Mr. Nash, and draws an impenetrable veil over his foibles. His singularities are forgotten when we behold his virtues, and he who laughed at the whimsical character of this Monarch of Bath, now laments that he is no more.

'BEAU' TALES

There are many colourful tales of Beau Nash's exploits, some apocryphal and some recounted by Nash himself – ad infinitum – in the bars and coffee-houses of Bath during his long twilight years. Oliver Goldsmith collected many of these stories told by, or about, Nash, in his biography: *A life of Richard Nash Esq.* The book also includes tales of his earlier student days, in which he already displayed an 'impenetrable assurance'.

One example recounts a bet that he won by riding naked through a village on a cow. Another, that on losing his last penny at the York races, he won £50 for standing outside York Minster as the congregation were filing out, wearing only a blanket. the Dean, who knew Nash, happened to chance by and asked him, *'What, Mr. Nash, in masquerade?'* Nash pointed to his companions who were watching close by and replied: *'No sir, only a Yorkshire penance for keeping bad company.'*

When still a law student, Nash chanced one day upon a poor man who was overheard to declare to his wife and large family of children, that ten pounds would make him happy. Nash gave him the money and later charged the sum to his legal society (of which he was treasurer), marking the entry *'For making one man happy – ten pounds'*. Oliver Goldsmith recounts that not only did the Inn make the payment, but doubled it!

The humiliation of being on the receiving end of Nash's sharp wit at a social occasion was often enough to deter transgressors. One habit he particularly frowned upon was the wearing of riding boots at the public assemblies. To get his point across to offenders Nash devised a puppet show in which Punch, booted and spurred, attempts to entice his mistress to bed. When she asks if he would mind removing his boots first, Punch replies: *'My boots! Why, madam, you may as well bid me pull off my legs. I never go without boots, I never ride, I never dance without them...'* and so on, until his impatient mistress ejects him from the stage. Any gentleman not catching the drift might be asked by Nash if he had *'forgot his horse'*. Few ventured to appear at the assemblies in riding dress after being humiliated in this way.

'BEAU' TALES

A riposte to a coffee-house gossip who had referred to Nash as a whoremonger: *'I acknowledge I have a woman living in my house, but if I do keep her, a man can no more be termed a whoremonger for having one whore in the house than a cheesemonger for having one cheese'*.

John Wesley, the founder of Methodism, unsurprisingly considered Bath an especially sinful place. In fact he described it as *'Satan's Throne'*. He was particularly concerned about the example the poor were being set by these pleasure-seeking aristocrats, governed by the profligate and over-dressed Nash. Nash, more concerned with social behaviour than questions of morality, believed that Wesley merely spread fear among the people. But Wesley was one of the few men able to match Nash's quick wit, as illustrated by the following incident:

One day close to the private chapel in Brock Street where Wesley sometimes preached, the two men came face to face. Nash blocked the preacher's path and told him, *'I never give way to fools.'* Wesley stepped off the pavement, doffed his hat and replied, *'However, Mr Nash, I do.'*

There is a tale that the Beau avenged himself by adding two french horns and some kettledrums to his orchestra, and parading them past one of Wesley's sermons playing *'God save the king'.*

It must be said that his humorous comments could occasionally be cruel:

On welcoming to the city a crippled woman, who informed him that she had come *'straight from London'*, he is said to have replied *'Confound me, Madam, then you must have been damnably warped on the way.'*

One wonders if he later regretted some of his more spontaneous outbursts of wit.

In his old age, and on a meagre pension provided by the City, Nash was unable to afford his mansion in St John's Court and moved to a less ostentatious house close by, where he lived out his last days tended by his one-time mistress, Juliana Papjoy. When Nash died, she is said to have resumed her life as a wandering herb-gatherer and, preferring not to live in a house again, slept in the bole of a dead tree.

RICHARD NASH: THE RULES OF CONDUCT

Nash compiled a list of rules to be observed at the public assemblies and had them posted up in the Pump Room for all new arrivals to the town to note – and take heed of!

RULES
by general Consent determined

1 That a visit of ceremony at coming to Bath, and another at going away, is all that is expected or desired by ladies of quality and fashion – except impertinents.

2 That ladies coming to the ball appoint a time for their footmen's coming to wait on them at home, to prevent disturbances and inconveniences to themselves and others.

3 That gentlemen of fashion never appear in a morning before the ladies in gowns or caps and shew breeding and respect.

4 That no person take it ill that anyone goes to another's play or breakfast, and not to their's – except captious by nature.

5 That no gentleman gives his tickets for the balls to any but gentle women – N.B. Unless he has none of his acquaintance.

6 That gentlemen crowding before ladies at the ball, shew ill-manners; and that none do so for the future – except such as respect nobody but themselves.

7 That no gentleman or lady take it ill that another dances before them – except such as have no pretence to dance at all.

8 That the elder ladies and children be contented with a second bench at the ball, as being past or not come to perfection.

9 That the younger ladies take notice how many eyes observe them –
N.B. This does not extend to the Have-at-alls.

10 That all whisperers of lies and scandal be taken for their authors.

11 That all repeaters of such lies and scandal be shunned by all company – except such as have been guilty of the same crime. N.B. Several men of no character, old women and young ones of questioned reputation, are great authors of lies in this place, being of the sect of Levellers.

RALPH ALLEN (1693-1764)

With Richard Nash shaping the new Bath society scene, the stage was set for the next phase of Bath's transformation. Enter Ralph Allen, the son of a Cornish inn-keeper, who, like Nash, had come to Bath seeking his fortune. But it was not the gaming-tables which attracted Allen. His perhaps equally unlikely route to fame and fortune was a job with the postal service.

Ralph Allen's own bid for glory came when in his official capacity as deputy postmaster, he intercepted letters from Jacobite rebels who, in opposition to the accession of the Hanoverian George I, sought to re-instate the Stuart line in the form of the 'Old Pretender', James Edward Stuart. The letters provided information about an illegal arms cache making its way to the West Country as part of a planned uprising. General Wade, at that time stationed in Bath, was notified, and in return for this valuable information, Wade helped Ralph Allen win a contract to run the country's provincial post – at the time a corrupt and inefficient system. Allen was able to thoroughly modernise the service, utilising the cross-post system whereby mail could be sent directly to its destination rather than being first sent to London to be sorted. In so doing Ralph Allen made the first of two fortunes.

Allen soon set his sights on new goals. He began quarrying the hitherto under-used limestone from Combe Down on the southern slopes of the city and devised an ingenious tramway to transport the stone in trucks down the steep hill from the quarries to the banks of the River Avon. From here Allen hoped to send the stone by ship to Bristol and to London – an ambition not as straight forward as it might have been: since the early Middle Ages the river had been too shallow for navigation on its approach from Bristol. This had occurred as a result of the river being dammed in order to harness power for the mills serving the wool industry.

Successive mill owners and other local merchants, fearing competition from Bristol and overseas markets, had resisted all attempts to rectify the problem. Only in 1727, with support from Ralph Allen, was an Avon Navigation Scheme completed. (It did, however, suffer some early setbacks – local coal-workers, concerned for their own livelihoods, sabotaged the lock at Saltford, four miles from Bath).

Allen was now able to transport his limestone to other cities, but his hopes of selling it in London were dashed when it was considered to be too soft for the capital's buildings. Despite this disappointment he soon found other uses for the newly navigable Avon. Turning his attention away from other markets he began to consider ideas for a large scale re-building programme for Bath itself. The quarry tramline enabled swift transportation of the stone to the city and the navigability of the Avon ensured that it could be supplied with sufficient quantities of timber, Welsh slates, iron and window-glass from Bristol. Equally importantly, the river could now provide an alternative means of access to the city for its visiting clientele at a time when travel by road could still be uncomfortable and sometimes dangerous.

All was in place for the dramatic visual transformation of the city. Allen needed only an architect with the vision and creativity to help him realise his ambition. This he found in John Wood.

JOHN WOOD THE ELDER (1704-1754)

John Wood, the only local man in the triumvirate of founding fathers of Bath, was not yet a pupil at the Bluecoat Charity School when Richard Nash made his first hopeful journey into the city in 1705. Little is known of Wood's early life and for many years it was believed that he was a native Yorkshireman, for it was in Yorkshire that he was working as a surveyor in 1725, when he received a plan of the city – possibly from Ralph Allen himself – which inspired him to formulate an audaciously ambitious scheme to rebuild Bath as a new Rome. This scheme was to provide the blueprint which would transform the cramped Medieval city into one of the architectural wonders of Europe.

In his book, *An Essay Towards a Description of Bath*, first published in 1742, Wood described the genesis of these early ideas:

When I found Work was likely to go on, I began to turn my Thoughts towards the Improvement of the City by Building; and for the Purpose I procured a Plan of the Town, which was sent me into Yorkshire, in the Summer of the Year 1725, where I, at my leisure Hours, formed one Design for the Ground, at the North West Corner of the City; and another for the Land, on the North East Side of the Town and River....In each Design, I proposed to make a grand Place of Assembly, to be called the Royal Forum of Bath; another Place, no less magnificent, for the exhibition of Sports, to be called the Grand Circus; and a third Place, of equal State with either of the former, for the Practice of medicinal Exercises, to be called the Imperial Gymnasium of the City, from a Work of that Kind, taking its Rise at first in Bath, during the Time of the Roman Emperors.

John Wood worked in the Classical Palladian style of architecture, which had seen a revival in the early 1700s as a reaction against the Baroque style associated with Christopher Wren and others. But his influences were far wider than a merely fashionable interest in Classical Rome. His passions included a serious (though not altogether scientific) study of prehistoric antiquities and of Celtic, particularly Druidic, culture. A devout Freemason, his identification of God as the 'Great Architect of the Universe' incorporated a belief that all classical architecture had its roots in Jewish antiquity. Wood thus surmised that Roman and Celtic building in Bath shared a common ancestor. A patriotic historicism and a deep affection for the city of his birth led him to unite these different and (to most modern observers) disparate cultural traditions into an authentic historical whole, much as scholars such as Geoffrey of Monmouth had attempted 600 years earlier. These ideas would find expression in some of his best work in the city and would imbue them with an almost mystical significance.

JOHN WOOD

To support some of his wilder antiquarian theories, John Wood claimed to have discovered (from what appears to be the scantiest of archaeological evidence) the remains of two prehistoric temples on Lansdown Hill on the northern slopes of Bath, one dedicated to the sun-goddess, known to the Druids as Bel, and another to the west of this, dedicated to Onca, the name the Phoenicians gave to the moon-goddess. Wood describes the sun temple in his *Essay on Bath:*

> *...as we ascend the Hill now bearing the Name of Lansdown, there are three large Stones lying upon the Ground, in a little Field by the Side of the Road, known by the Name of Sols Rocks, with a Foundation just behind them, shaped into a Circular Form...These three Stones, when erect and perfect, seem to have made a stupendous Altar; and the circular Foundation behind them seems to have borne other erect Stones, which, in all Probability, were set up by King Bladud for a Temple in honour of the Sun.*

If these structures had indeed existed, they would surely have provided the inspiration behind the Romans' own temples to Sol and Luna in Aquae Sulis, but there appears to be no other evidence to suggest the validity of his claims.

John Wood returned to live in Bath in 1727 with an opportunity to create the kind of dramatic architectural impact on Bath that only the Romans, and perhaps John de Villula, had achieved before him. He launched into the task at hand with a conviction bordering on obsession.

But John Wood was to find little encouragement from the City Fathers, who were deeply suspicious of his grandiose schemes. The Corporation owned much of the land within the city walls, and therefore could, and most often did, veto his radical designs.

Much of the area immediately outside the city walls, however, was in private ownership. As Bath came under pressure for suitable building land, the landowners needed only to be convinced that the city's popularity could be sustained. And so began the long and often frustrating task of winning round the wealthy landowners to his plans.

There had already been a small amount of speculative building within the city and John Wood knew well how the market worked. Once he had succeeded in leasing a plot of land, he would subdivide it into smaller house-sized plots and sub-let these to local builders. The external features of each house would conform strictly to his design, but behind each façade, contractors were free to choose their own internal layouts.

JOHN WOOD

John Wood's health declined rapidly in the last years of his life, and an increased urgency to see his vision fully realised only served to deepen the intransigence which had been partly responsible for the thwarting of many of his architectural ambitions. He was to receive no major civic commission in the Georgian city which he had helped create. Yet even the rivalry he provoked with other architects helped to push the expansion of the city more rapidly, as each of them strived to emulate or surpass the splendour of his designs.

He had completed much of his major work in the city by the age of thirty, and died in 1754 without witnessing the completion of what many consider to be his masterpiece: The King's Circus. His obituary notice in the Bath Chronicle stated:

Amidst a world of Calumnies, Falsehoods and Discouragements, which he bravely surmounted: He not only raised himself in the Esteem of his Superiors: but in the Compass of a few Years, by an honesty and commendable Industry, obtain'd an handsome Competence for himself and Family – In a word, he had no enemies but those who either envied him Themselves, or went too far in crediting the defamatory Reproaches and Scandals of Others.'

QUEEN SQUARE

John Wood's first major undertaking in Bath was Queen Square. Designed in 1728 and completed in 1736, the palace-like façade of the north-side displays English Palladian architecture at its most confident.

THE QUEEN SQUARE GARDEN

The square enclosed a formal garden of gravel walks and ordered green spaces. Wood designed the area to be a place of assembly: *'For the Intention of a Square in a City, is for People to assemble together; and the Spot whereon they meet, ought to be separated from the Ground common to Men and Beasts, and even to Mankind in General, if Decency and good order are to be observed in such Places of Assembly.'*

THE QUEEN SQUARE OBELISK

Commissioned by Richard Nash and designed by John Wood the Elder, the obelisk in Queen Square was erected in 1738 to commemorate the visit of Frederick, Prince of Wales. The inscription on the south-side of the obelisk was written by Alexander Pope, and reads:
In Memory
Of Honours Conferr'd
And in Gratitude,
For Benefits Bestow'd
In this City,
By His Royal Highness
Frederick,
Prince of Wales,
And His
Royal Consort,
In the Year
MDCCXXXVIII.
This Obelisk is Erected
By Richard Nash, Esq.

THE CIRCUS. Designed by John Wood the Elder, 1754. Completed by
John Wood the Younger, 1770.

THE KING'S CIRCUS

The King's Circus, now simply known as the Circus, was the architectural creation in which John Wood's fascination with Celtic and Roman antiquity found its most perfect expression. It is said to have been partly inspired by the Colosseum at Rome, but designed to be seen from within – '*Vespasian's amphitheatre turned outside in*' as Smollett's Matthew Bramble describes it, in the novel, *Humphry Clinker.*

The Circus forms a perfect circle with three equally spaced approaches dividing three arcs of ten houses each. The design of the interior is constant throughout its 360 degrees: rows of columns showing the three principal orders of classical architecture, one on top of the other: *Doric* on the ground floor; *Ionic* at first-floor level and *Corinthian* on the second floor.

Over the doorways a decorative frieze runs all the way around each arc depicting, in its 525 metopes, symbols from a somewhat baffling array of subjects. John Wood adapted these designs from a number of different sources including illustrations featured in a seventeenth century book of poems by George Withers, called *A collection of Emblemes Ancient and Moderne.*

Less immediately obvious than its debt to classical styles is the respect Wood paid to Bath's Druidic heritage, the details of which suggest less of an inspirational debt to the Roman Amphitheatre, and more of a celebration of his abiding fascination with the stone circles at Stonehenge and Stanton Drew. Wood based the dimensions of the Circus upon his own calculations of the outer circles of the ancient monuments. Hence the number of houses in the Circus corresponds to the number of individual standing stones he calculated to be in the prehistoric circles. For a time it was even believed that the Circus contained three approaches only because Wood had been working from a seventeenth century plan of Stonehenge, a drawing which was later revealed to have erroneously included two farm tracks of more recent origin. Had Wood been aware of this, the Circus may well have had just one approach – from the south.

THE CIRCUS

Close inspection of the Circus buildings reveal many fascinating details of John Wood's cross-fertilising of ideas. His attachment to the Bladud Legend, for example, is exhibited in the stone acorns which crown the parapets astride double Corinthian columns: an allusion to the first King of Bath's discovery of the springs and the druidic significance of the region. The druids were known as the 'Priests of the Hollow Oak' (the word druid derives from the Greek word 'drus', meaning oak). John Wood may well have intended the double Corinthian column to represent the Hollow Oak; the acorn to symbolise the Druid priest. He would no doubt also have been aware of yet another of the Saxon names for the town:

Akemeanster, and of its possible interpretation as 'The Place of the Oak'.

The Circus contains 648 columns of the classical orders: Doric, Ionic and Corinthian. The frieze, supported by Doric columns at ground floor level, depicts symbols from a wide range of subjects in the arts and sciences, including: heraldry, weapons, Masonic signs, mathematical instruments, serpents, winged hearts and tragic masks.

The Circus enclosure was originally cobbled and the central area, where now stand tall London plane trees, contained a covered reservoir which supplied the houses with water. (Not pumped directly of course, but collected in pails by servants!)

In 1967 **No.1 the Royal Crescent** was given to the Bath Preservation Trust. The house, open to the public in the spring and summer, has been restored and furnished as it would have looked in the Georgian period.

THE ROYAL CRESCENT

John Wood the Elder is rightly credited with being the driving force behind the extraordinary metamorphosis of the city's architecture in the eighteenth century, but his son (also John) was without question a talented and methodical architect in his own right. Wood the Younger was responsible for overseeing most of the construction of the Circus (his father died only three months after the foundation stone was laid) and went on to design many other important buildings in Bath, including the Upper Assembly Rooms in 1771.

He is often credited with the design of the Royal Crescent, but it seems more probable that the structure was intended as part of John Wood the Elder's vision for the north-east quadrant of the town, which included the Circus. It provides one last twist in the tale of the elder Wood's abiding fixation with ancient cultures, and centres around the Druid's historic reputation as master astronomers. In Classical Palladian architecture the Ionic form is associated with the moon, and is represented in the Royal Crescent with its single line of Ionic columns. A more obvious clue lies in the crescent shape itself – never previously used in English house design, yet vital to Wood's scheme. If one thinks back to the shape of the Circus, Wood's intentions become clearer: he had visualised architectural representations of the sun and the moon on the Lansdown slopes where, he believed, Bladud had once built temples dedicated to Bel and Onca.

The influence of the stone circles is there too in the thirty houses which make up the curve of the Crescent.

And so it appears that the Woods' two greatest architectural achievements in Bath, rightly recognised and admired throughout the world, owe less to the inspiration of the Classical world and more to a celebration of the traditions of its pagan ancestors.

THE ROYAL CRESCENT

The Royal Crescent, completed in 1775 by John Wood the
Younger, comprises a curve of thirty houses linked by 114 Ionic
columns at first-floor level. Over 50 feet in height and 500 feet
long, its wide pavement and cobbled roadway are fronted by a
gently sloping lawn.

When first constructed, Bath's most famous architectural
creation was bounded on three sides by open countryside; the only
street approach being from the east. Its position – set back slightly
from the road – served to maximise the visual impact of the curve
of the crescent as one turned the corner from Brock Street.

The Royal Crescent presented visitors entering the city from the
west along the River Avon with their first striking views of the
Georgian architecture of Bath.

THE ROYAL CRESCENT LAWN

The Crescent lawn marked a move away from the more formal
garden design which characterised John Wood the Elder's work in
Queen's Square, reflecting the influence of the Lancelot 'Capability'
Brown school of 'studied nature' in landscape design.

Separating the lawn from what is now part of the Royal Victoria
Park, a low stone wall with a ditch behind it, constructed so as to
be invisible from the Crescent itself, gives the impression of a
much larger lawn area. The construction known as a *'ha-ha'* was
built to prevent sheep from invading the well-tended grass of the
Crescent lawn. Its name may derive from the amusement of
watching those unaware of its presence tumbling over it into the
ditch below.

No. 30 The Royal Crescent.

THE ROYAL CRESCENT

As Bath grew increasingly fashionable in the eighteenth century, the city attracted regular visits from the famous. One such luminary was the composer Franz Joseph Haydn, who recorded his impressions of Bath in one of his notebooks during a second visit to the city, in 1794:

Bath is one of the most beautiful cities in Europe. All the houses are built of stone; this stone comes from quarries in the surrounding mountains; it is very white. The whole city lies on a slope and that is why there are very few carriages: instead of them there are a lot sedan chairs, who will take you quite a way for six-pence. But too bad there are so few straight roads; there are a lot of beautiful squares, on which stand the most magnificent houses, but which cannot be reached by any vehicle.

Today, on the the 3rd, I looked at the city, and found, half-way up the hill, a building shaped like a half-moon and more magnificent than any I had seen in London. The curve extends for 100 fathoms and there is a corinthian column at each fathom.

The city is not thickly populated, and in the Summer one sees very few people; for the people taking the baths don't come till the beginning of October, and stay through half of February. The baths by nature are very warm; one bathes in the water, and one always drinks it – generally better the latter.

Franz Joseph Haydn from his *Collected Correspondence and London Notebooks.* Volume 111, August 1794

PRIOR PARK

Ralph Allen's disappointment at having his Bath stone rejected by the London markets, gave him the spur he needed to plan his great country mansion at Prior Park. As John Wood explains in his *Essay towards a description of Bath*: *'The Reflections cast upon the Free Stone of the hills of Bath, brought Allen to a Resolution to exhibit it in a Seat which he had determined to build for himself near his Works, to much greater Advantage, and in much great Variety of Uses than it had ever appeared in any other structure'.*

Unbound by the constraints of the established landed gentry Ralph Allen was free to build his family estate in whatever style he wished in the city where he had made his fortune. It is unsurprising then, that his country mansion was Palladian architecture at its grandest, and that its position overlooking the town provided, as Phillip Thicknesse observed (not altogether charitably one would guess): *'...a noble seat, which sees all Bath and which was built, probably, for all Bath to see'.* Acclaimed by the renowned authority on Georgian architecture, Walter Ison, as *'one of the finest expressions of Palladian ideals and principles ever achieved in this country'*, when complete it was as Allen had intended it to be: a potent advertisement for the qualities of Bath stone.

PRIOR PARK

John Wood the Elder was responsible for the original design of the house at Prior Park, but it was completed in 1741 by Allen's Clerk of Works, Richard Jones, after Allen and Wood fell out over details of the project.

THE PALLADIAN BRIDGE

Over time Ralph Allen added a number of unusual features to his Prior Park Estate including a Gothic temple, sham bridge and a serpentine lake. The predictability of the formal garden was gradually superceded by a landscape of 'visual surprises'. Alexander Pope described this approach to garden design in the rhyming couplets:

Let not each beauty everywhere be spied
When half the skill is decently to hide.
He gains all points who pleasingly confounds,
Surprises, varies and conceals the bounds.

The most impressive of these visual surprises is the Palladian Bridge. Based on a drawing by Andrea Palladio, and completed around 1755, it stands over an ornamental pool in the lower area of the deer park, where the priory monks once kept ponds well-stocked with carp.

AT PRIOR PARK

The popularity of Bath as a fashionable watering-hole brought an influx of artists and writers into the city in the hope of finding a rich source of inspiration and patronage for their work. Ralph Allen was a generous benefactor, especially of writers, for whom he had a particular respect. Prior Park soon became famed for its artistic and literary connections.

Among the many celebrated and distinguished guests at Allen's house, were the painters Thomas Gainsborough and William Hoare; the author Samuel Richardson and the leading actor of his day, David Garrick, with whom Allen kept a regular correspondence for some years.

Ralph Allen's benevolence, often praised (not surprisingly perhaps) by the writers whom he generously patronised, inevitably led to his being eulogised in poems and novels of the day: Henry Fielding, who was himself a regular visitor to the Allen household, portrayed him as Squire Allen in his novel *Tom Jones:*

Neither Mr Allworthy's house nor his heart were shut against any part of mankind, but they were both more particularly open to men of merit. To say the truth, this was the only house in the kingdom where you were sure to gain a dinner by deserving it.

Above all others, men of genius and learning shared the principal place in his favour, and in those he had much discernment; for though he had missed the advantage of a learned education, yet being blessed with vast natural abilities, he had so well profited by a vigorous, though late application to letters, and by much conversation with men of eminence in this way, that he was himself a very competent judge in most kinds of literature.

When Fielding died, at the age of 47, it is said that Allen paid for his children to complete their education.

Alexander Pope was another regular visitor to Prior Park, and assisted Allen in the designs for his garden. A 'wilderness area' on the estate has been credited to the poet. Pope praised his sometime benefactor in the rhyming couplet:

Let humble Allen, with an awkward shame,
Do good by stealth and blush to find it fame.

The ancestral seat did not, however, stay long in the Allen family: after Ralph Allen's death there was a succession of different owners, and gradually the house and gardens fell into decay. Today the landscape garden is owned by the National Trust and has been restored to its former glory.

The Mansion and Palladian Bridge at Prior Park

THE PRIOR PARK LANDSCAPE GARDEN

Once the estate of the Benedictine priory (seized by the Crown after the dissolution of the monasteries), the extensive grounds of Prior Park formed part of the Prior's deer park. The garden, which cascades down the hillside almost to the banks of the River Avon, was to undergo several stages in its development under Ralph Allen's stewardship, reflecting changing fashions in garden design during the eighteenth century. The more formal garden of straight lines, walks and rides, which had characterised the work of earlier architects, gave way to landscape design which exhibited a greater appreciation of natural beauty. *'All art consists in the imitation and study of nature',* was to be the creed of designers such as Lancelot 'Capability' Brown, who were creating landscapes of 'studied naturalism'.

Henry Fielding described Prior Park as a place where:

Nature appears in her richest attire, and art dressed with modest simplicity attends her benignent mistress. Here nature indeed pours forth the choicest treasure which she hath lavished on this world.

SHAM CASTLE

Not a real castle, but an imposing castellated wall, high up on Claverton Down. Built in 1762, the design has been attributed to Richard Jones, Ralph Allen's Clerk of Works. The only real function the 'castle' served was as an advertisement for Allen's stone quarries.

OLIVER GOLDSMITH AND
THE BATH SEASON

In his biography of Richard Nash, Oliver
Goldsmith provides one of the most lucid and
entertaining portraits of Bath at the height of
its fashion in the eighteenth century.

The author of *She stoops to conquer* and *The
Vicar of Wakefield* describes Bath's rise from a
town of *'bucolic charm, splenetic, rustic and
vulgar'*, to a resort for the aristocratic,
cultivated and wealthy – The *'quality'*. The
'Bath Season' soon lasted throughout the
winter months, and by the end of the century
Bath guide books warned that the expensive
months lasted from September to May.

Goldsmith describes the pleasures of the
social round at Bath:

*Upon a stranger's arrival at Bath, he is
welcomed by a peal of the abbey bells, and in
the next place by the voice and music of the city
waits. For these civilities, the ringers have
generally a present made them of half-a-guinea,
and the waits of half-a-crown, or more, in
proportion to the person's fortune, generosity, or
ostentation...After the family is thus welcomed
to Bath, it is the custom for the master of it to
go to the public places, and subscribe two
guineas at the assembly houses towards the
balls and music in the pump-house, for which
he is entitled to three tickets every ball night.
His next subscription is a crown, half-a-guinea,
or a guinea, according to his rank and quality,
for the liberty of walking in the private walks
belonging to Simpson's assembly house; a
crown or half-a-guinea is also given to the
booksellers, for which the gentleman is to have
what books he pleases to read at his lodgings,
and at the coffee-house another subscription is
taken for pen, ink, and paper, for such letters
as the subscriber shall write at it during his
stay. The ladies, too, may subscribe to the
booksellers, and to a house by the pump-room,
for the advantage of reading the news, and for
enjoying each other's conversation.*

OLIVER GOLDSMITH AND
THE BATH SEASON

*...the amusements of the day are generally
begun by bathing, which is no unpleasant
method of passing away an hour or so...The
hours of bathing are commonly between six and
nine in the morning, and the baths are every
morning supplied with fresh water...The
amusement of bathing is immediately
succeeded by a general assembly of people at
the pump-house, some for pleasure, and some
to drink the hot waters. Three glasses at three
different times is the usual portion for every
drinker; and the intervals between every glass
is enlivened by the harmony of a small band of
music, as well as by the conversation of the
gay, the witty, or the forward. From the pump-
house the ladies, from time to time, withdraw to
a female coffee house, and from thence return
to their lodgings for breakfast. The gentlemen
withdraw to their coffee houses to read the
papers, or converse on the news of the day with
a freedom and ease not to be found in the
metropolis....Thus we have the tedious morning
fairly over. When noon approaches, the church
(if any please to go there) is done, some of the
company appear on the parade, and other
public walks, where they continue to chat and
amuse each other, till they have formed parties
for the play, cards, or dancing for the evening.
Some walk in the meadows around the town,
while others are seen scaling those romantic
precipices that overhang the city...*

*Another part of the company divert
themselves with reading in the booksellers'
shops, or are generally seen taking the air and
exercise, some on horseback, some in coaches.
Some walk in the meadows round the town,
winding along the side of the river Avon....After
dinner is over, and evening prayers ended, the
company meet a second time at the pump-
house. From this they retire to the walks, and
thence go to drink tea at the assembly houses,
and the rest of the evenings are concluded
either with balls, plays or visits... Thus Bath
yields a continued rotation of diversions, and
people of all ways of thinking, even from the
libertine to the methodist, have it in their power
to complete the day with employment suited to
their inclinations.*

*Oliver Goldsmith
from The Life Of Richard Nash Of Bath,
Esq. 1762*

CHRISTOPHER ANSTEY AND
THE NEW BATH GUIDE

Christopher Anstey lived in the Royal Crescent for some years and was the author of the highly successful book *The New Bath Guide,* published in 1766. A witty, satirical observation of the Bath social scene, written in a series of versed letters, its protaganist, Simkin Blunderhead, is not so enamoured of the welcoming peal of bells:

...No city, dear Mother, this city excels
In charming sweet sounds both of fiddles and bells
I thought, like a fool, that they only would ring
For a wedding, or judge, or the birth of a King;
But I found 'twas for me that the good-natured people
Rung so hard that I thought they would pull down the steeple;
So I took out my purse, as I hate to be shabby,
And paid all the men when they came from the abbey;
Yet some think it strange they should make such a riot
In a place where sick folk would be glad to be quiet:
But I hear 'tis the business of this corporation
To welcome in all the great men of the nation;
For you know there is nothing diverts or employs
The minds of great people like making a noise;
So with bells they contrive all as much as they can
To tell the arrival of any such man.
If a broker, or statesman, a gamester, or peer,
a naturalised Jew, or a bishop, come here,
Or an eminent trader in cheese should retire
Just to think of the business the State may require;
With horns and with trumpets, with fiddles and drums
They'll strive to divert him as soon as he comes;
'Tis amazing to find such a number of ways
Of employing his thoughts all the time that he stays:
If by chance the great man at his lodging alone is
He may view from his window the collier's ponies
On both the Parades, where they tumble and kick,
To the great entertainment of those that are sick:
What a number of turnspits and builders he'll find
For relaxing his cares and unbending his mind;
While notes of sweet music contend with the cries
Of 'fine potted laver, fresh oysters, and pies!'
And music's a thing I shall truly revere,
Since the city musicians so tickle my ear:
For when we arrived here at Bath t'other day,
They came to our lodgings on purpose to play.

BATH BOOKSELLERS

An increase in literacy among the new middle classes in the eighteenth century led to more and more published material being available. This was the great age of the novel and, with licensing regulations abolished, a proliferation of newspapers reflected a growing interest in world affairs. Periodicals, which had made their first appearance at the beginning of the century, soon became a useful source of advertising for spa towns such as Bath.

The booksellers that Goldsmith describes in his book *The life of Richard Nash*, were as much libraries and reading rooms as bookshops. In them, one could browse the London newspapers and local papers such as the Bath Chronicle – which is still circulated today.

Charges for subscription were a guinea for a nobleman, and five shillings for a commoner. An extra fee was charged for use of pens and writing paper.

Lydia Melford in Smollett's *Humphry Clinker,* described them as: *'these charming places of resort',* where one could *'read novels, plays, pamphlets and newspapers for so small a subscription as a crown a quarter; and in these offices of intelligence, as my brother calls them, all the reports of the day and all the private transactions of the Bath, are first entered and discussed...'*

THE WINDOW TAX

First levied in 1691, and greatly increased in 1782, the window tax was intended as a tax on wealth: it presumed that the bigger the house you lived in, the more windows it was likely to have. In the 1740s an amendment to the tax was introduced which stated that if two windows were less than 12 inches apart they counted as one. The obvious solution – quickly seized upon by Bath residents – was to move the windows closer together. An alternative was simply to block the windows up altogether, as can still be seen in some houses in Bath.

The law was repealed in 1851, after the Crystal Palace – a building made almost entirely of glass – was erected for the Great Exhibition.

The Bookseller's Window.
A convincing 'trompe l'oeil' in Grove Street.

SALLY LUNN'S HOUSE

Situated in what was once known as Lilliput Alley, Sally Lunn's is reputed to be one of the oldest houses in Bath. Excavations have revealed evidence of a Roman dwelling 5 feet below the current cellar floor – a reminder that the settlement lay up to 15 feet beneath the present city level. The Roman house would have stood a short, level distance from the gently sloping banks of the River Avon.

Above the Roman remains, evidence of medieval occupation has also been unearthed, including a faggot oven. Given its location, it is possible that the oven was used to prepare food for the masons building the Norman cathedral in the eleventh and twelth centuries.

Sally Lunn herself is thought to have been a Huguenot refugee who came to work in the bakery around 1680, bringing with her the recipe for the confectionery which has become associated with her name.

A slightly more prosaic explanation for the origin of the Sally Lunn reminds us that the French have always known this kind of bun as a *'Sol et Lune'*, because it is yellow on top and white underneath. Sally Lunn may simply be an anglicised version of the French name.

The original recipe, thought to have been lost, was rediscovered behind a panel over the medieval fireplace in the 1930s.

THE UPPER ASSEMBLY ROOMS

The expansion of the city to the north-west, made possible by the Woods' speculative building schemes, was crowned in 1775 by the completion of the Royal Crescent. The area was soon established unquestionably as the fashionable quarter of town. The two assembly rooms close to the Abbey were looking increasingly remote from this northward migration of Bath Society, and their position an inconvenience to the new residents of the Upper Town. When new assembly rooms close to the Circus were completed in 1771, the Lower Rooms found it hard to compete. One closed almost immediately and the other struggled to retain its clientele.

Inevitably a tension developed between the Upper and Lower Towns, with the city-centre looking increasingly antiquated in comparison with the spanking-new white crescents and squares flaunting themselves on the sunny south-facing slopes of Lansdown.

The City finally galvanised into action and set about rebuilding the still largely medieval town centre. Changes included large-scale development of the Pump Rooms, the Cross and Hot Baths and demolition of the confusion of narrow Saxon lanes which had previously linked them.

The Upper Assembly Rooms, designed by John Wood the Younger, and completed in 1771.

THE FIRST PUMP ROOM: 1706

By the beginning of the eighteenth century, the drinking of the spa waters was firmly established, and with the numbers of visitors to the town rising each year, it became urgent that the City provide a more comfortable means of taking the cure than the 'alfresco' arrangement which had hitherto existed. Among those who petitioned for a pump-room to be built, was Dr William Oliver, insisting that one of the worst accidents that could happen to anybody in the course of drinking the waters was to catch a chill. (Dr Oliver's fame lives on as the inventor of the Bath Oliver; a dry wafer-like biscuit which the doctor prescribed as part of his treatments.)

With money raised by Richard Nash, Dr Oliver and other Bath physicians, a pump-room was built on land to north of the King's Bath, which soon became a popular meeting-place. A song to Bladud was specially composed for the opening ceremony in 1706.

It was not long before some London physicians began to view the development of the provincial spa town as a threat to their own lucrative livelihoods. The eminent Dr John Radcliffe took such a dislike to the city that he threatened to poison the Bath waters by casting a toad into the spring. Beau Nash was able to calm any worries visitors might have of such a mishap by hiring a group of six professional musicians to play in the Pump Room daily, saying he would charm the toad as one would charm the venom from a tarantula – with music: *'I will fiddle the amphibious creatures out of the hot waters; and, by the power of harmony, charm every one on whom the toad should spit his poison into such a dance as should drive out the venom and turn languishment into gaiety.'*

Opinions on the taste of the water vary: Celia Fiennes, providing one of the more evocative descriptions, considered that it:

tastes like the water that boyles Eggs, has such a smell, but the nearer the pumpe you drinke it, the hotter and less offensive and more spiriteous.

The Bath Guide of 1800 advised that:

The water should always be drank hot from the pump, or else at your lodgings as warm as it can possibly be procured...The water is generally drank in the morning fasting, between the hours of six and ten, that it may have time to pass out of the stomach; though some drink a glass about noon.

The quantity generally taken in a day is from one pint to three, though some drink two quarts; few constitutions require more.'

THE ROYAL MINERAL HOSPITAL

The number of impoverished and dispossessed sick seeking refuge in the city continued to increase in the early part of the eighteenth century. In an effort to control the numbers, and yet provide proper facilities for those who *were* admitted, local dignitaries began, in 1716, the task of raising funds for a new free hospital to care for '..*poor lepers, cripples, and other indigent persons resorting to Bath for a cure...and to discriminate real objects of charity from vagrants and other impostors who crowd both the church and the town to the annoyance of the gentry residing there.*' It was stipulated that they could not be treated unless they had a certificate of recommendation from their parish and three pounds to pay for their return journey. If they were not cured the money paid for their burial.

Sponsors and benefactors included Dr Oliver and Beau Nash. Ralph Allen provided the stone free from his quarries, and John Wood donated his services as architect. The hospital, completed in 1742, was situated close to the medieval north wall, at a comfortable distance from the then fashionable quarter of town which centred around Terrace Walk and the two Assembly Rooms. Linked to the Hot Bath by narrow Saxon lanes, its inmates were segregated as far as was possible from the pleasure-seeking elite.

The Royal Mineral Water Hospital (now known as the Royal National Hospital for Rheumatic Diseases), continues to treat people from all over the country (patients, however, are no longer obliged to provide evidence of enough cash to get home again).

Dr. Oliver examining patients. From the painting by William Hoare in the Royal National Hospital for Rheumatic Diseases.
Appointed physician to the Royal Mineral Water Hospital in 1740, Dr Oliver was the author of a book published in 1751, entitled, *A Practical Essay on the Use and Abuse of warm Bathing in Gouty Cases.*

THE GREAT PUMP ROOM: 1796.

By the end of the eighteenth century the first Pump Room had been replaced by a new complex designed by two prominent Bath architects of the day, Thomas Baldwin and John Palmer. This scheme formed part of a large-scale development of the Baths and the area west of Stall Street, involving the demolition of the maze of Saxon lanes which had linked the Pump Room to the Cross Bath and the Hot Bath. In their place, five new streets were constructed, including Bath Street, with its colonnaded pavements, which led from a renovated Cross Bath to a new west facing entrance of the Pump Room in Stall Street. The Hot Bath was rebuilt in 1777 by John Wood the Younger – his last major work in the city, and the only civic commission he ever received.

A colonnade to the north of the new Pump Room entrance, completed in 1786 by Baldwin, led to the Abbey Court Yard and to a new concert room, which stood between the Pump Room and the Abbey. The new arrangements made it possible to walk from the Cross Bath through to the Abbey almost entirely under cover.

It was during the construction of this second Pump Room that parts of the pediment from the Roman Temple of Sulis Minerva first came to light, although further exploration had to wait until 1867.

The Stall Street entrance to the **Great Pump Room,** designed by Thomas Baldwin and completed in 1796 by John Palmer.

LANSDOWN CRESCENT

Development in the north-west of the city continued unabated in the last quarter of the eighteenth century, despite serious financial setbacks caused by the American War of Independence and the Napoleonic Wars. The steeper slopes of Lansdown presented new difficulties for architects, in which the strict rules of Palladian symmetry could not always be applied. Being forced to work much more *with* the landscape gave scope for the kind of visual surprises which Alexander Pope had sought in garden design.

Lansdown Crescent, designed by John Palmer and completed in 1792, comprises a long double curve of houses closely following the contours of the hillside. At each end of the main terrace, curved sections with bow windows create the effect of architectural book-ends. Narrow lanes separate the terrace from the undulating curves of Lansdown Place East and Lansdown Place West, which flank the crescent. The serpentine configuration is picked up again a little further to the west in the arc of Somerset Place, designed by John Eveleigh, another of the talented architects working in Bath in the last great phase of its development.

Lansdown Crescent, looking out over a steeply sloping lawn, has far more dramatic visual impact than the lawn fronting the Royal Crescent, and marks a departure from the gentler prospects of the 'Capability' Brown school, towards the Picturesque movement in landscape gardening.

Lansdown Crescent designed by John Palmer, 1792

SEDAN CHAIRS AND LINK SNUFFERS

As the new squares and terraces marched their way up the Lansdown slopes year by year, the job for sedan chair carriers, who had the unenviable task of transporting the wealthy inhabitants to and from social engagements, grew ever harder (and ever more lucrative). The sedan chair, essentially a large, covered box, carried by means of horizontal bars fastened to its sides, was, in an age before the motor car, the only convenient and (relatively) comfortable means of transportation available. Although the chairmen themselves were sometimes guilty of making it anything but comfortable, as in the case of the General, described by John Wood, who was, *'kept prisoner in a Chair, with the Top lifted up, in a hard, rainy Night, till he was as Wet as if he had been immersed in Water'*.

It was Richard Nash who ensured that proper licensing and a fixed scale of fees, was introduced. Still, there can be little doubt that the chairmen earned their money; a journey from the Pump Rooms to the Lansdown Crescent, for instance, would necessitate some back-breakingly steep climbs. The city may have been a place of rest and healing for some, but probably did little to extend the lives of its sedan chairmen! Charles Dickens, in his novel *Pickwick Papers*, describes a rather ill-matched pair: *'Just as the clock struck three, there was blown into the Crescent a sedan chair with Mr Dowler inside, borne by one short, fat chairman, and one long, thin one, who had much ado to keep their bodies perpendicular; to say nothing of the chair.'*

LINK SNUFFERS
Ahead of the sedans walked the link-boys carrying lighted torches called links. Once their charges had been deposited safely home, the links were extinguished in hollow metal cones called 'snuffers'. Snuffers can still be seen at the entrances to some of the houses on Lansdown Crescent.

THE PULTENEY BRIDGE, designed by Robert Adam in 1770, was inspired by the Ponte Vecchio in Florence. Until its completion, a ferry guided by an overhead rope provided the only means of crossing the river to the Bathwick Meadows.

90

THE PULTENEY BRIDGE

In the 1760s, proposals were made for the most ambitious neo-classical development the city had seen so far. The site was to be the Bathwick Estate, an area of flat meadow land (a rare commodity in Bath) on the east banks of the Avon, owned by Sir Richard Pulteney. Plans were tendered by Robert Adam, one of the most influential architects of his day, and one of the few architects to work in the city during this period who was not a local man. His plans included the construction of a new bridge close to the point of the original Roman river-crossing which, since the damming of the river in the late Saxon period to provide power for the wool mills, had been replaced by a ferry guided by an overhead rope. Ultimately, only Adam's designs for the Pulteney Bridge were ever realised, as the American War of Independence saw investment withdrawn from the building market and re-directed towards the war effort. His plans for the rest of the estate were dropped and a less ambitious scheme by Thomas Baldwin, begun in 1788, saw the completion of Pulteney Street, Henrietta Street and Bathwick Street, before the French Revolution caused a further slump in the market and the bankruptcy of many developers – including Baldwin.

In some lights, the normally white or grey Bath stone can appear honey-coloured, as in this view of the **Pulteney Bridge.**

THE GUILDHALL

There has been a Guildhall on the present site since 1625, although the area in which it stands had long been a bustling market place for Bath's local traders. The Guildhall represented the power of the merchant guilds, that controlled and managed trades and crafts in the Middle Ages, reflecting Bath's continuing importance as a market town.

Intrigue and a hint of corruption surrounded the design and construction of the present building in the 1770s. Two local architects, Thomas Attwood and John Palmer, had submitted plans, but Attwood, who held a number of influential posts in the city, including City Architect, had received the commission over the proposals of Palmer, who had offered to do the job in return for leases on the shops and houses which would be part of the project. The story developed a further twist when, in 1775, Attwood was killed after a floor collapsed in a house he was surveying. The job then went to his assistant Thomas Baldwin, who revised Atwood's designs – even though work on construction had already begun.

Only the central frontage is by Baldwin; the wings and central dome were added by John Mackean Brydon in 1893. Their ornamental features, although a departure from the strict Palladian style of most 18th-century architecture in the city, blend well with the original design, whilst adding a touch of a more ornate style to a prominent city building.

To the north of the main building lies the Guildhall market. Just inside the entrance which faces the High Street, is a table-like stone called the 'nail', upon which local traders once struck their bargains. Once a deal had been agreed, the purchaser put his cash on the 'nail' and the transaction was sealed. The expression; 'paying on the nail', meaning to pay cash at the time of purchase, comes from the use of this stone.

REBECCA AT THE WELL

The statue of Rebecca at the Well, was erected in 1861 by the Temperance Association. The busy market place it once faced, contained numerous drinking establishments, hence the cautionary words inscribed on its base: WATER IS BEST.
The statue now faces the south wing of the Guildhall by J.M. Brydon, with its baroque frieze and cupola.

THE BATH OF JANE AUSTEN

The population of Bath when Richard Nash first set foot in the city in 1705, was around 2000. At the time of his death in 1761, it was 10,000, and by 1800 it had risen to 34,000. Ironically, as the nineteenth century dawned, the city was entering the twilight of its fashionable era, for it was fast losing the very quality which had made it popular with the leisured classes – its exclusivity. The nobility and gentry had begun to look elsewhere for amusement, to other spas and particularly the seaside towns such as Brighton. Those who did still come for the season avoided the arranged social occasions, now cheapened for them by the attendance of social climbers hoping, (with less and less likelihood) to rub shoulders with the rich and famous. The 'Quality' withdrew to what Jane Austen called the 'stupidity of private parties'. A state of affairs that Richard Nash would certainly not have allowed had he still been alive.

The type of new resident the city was attracting was also contributing to its decline; the rise in population being more and more accounted for by those seeking respectable retirement in the town. As its vitality drained away, Bath entered a long period of 'shabby gentility'. The city was described at the time, with a no doubt unintentional attempt at parodying its ecclesiastical past, as *'a sort of great monastery, inhabited by single people, particularly superannuated females.'* It was in this twilight of Bath's hey-day, that Jane Austen (perhaps uncomfortably close to fitting this description herself) came to live with her family when her father retired in 1801.

Jane Austen had visited Bath on a number of occasions before her extended stay from 1801-1805 and completed one novel, *Northanger Abbey,* in which the town played a significant role. But deriving creative inspiration from the occasional welcome visit, and being uprooted from her childhood home in Hampshire, were two different things. When told of her father's intentions to move the family to Bath, she is said to have passed out. It seemed an inauspicious sign that this would not be a happy change for her. And so it proved to be. Her feelings for the town were not improved by the reduced circumstances the family found themselves in, the numerous changes of address and, in 1805, the death of her father. It is perhaps no wonder that when she left the city for the last time, it was with *'happy feelings of escape.'*

NORTHANGER ABBEY

The detached view of the city which Jane Austen enjoyed during the writing of *Northanger Abbey* makes the novel a more frivolous study of manners and morals than her later 'Bath' novel, *Persuasion*. On arriving in the city, the young heroine, Catherine Morland, *'was all eager delight; – her eyes here, there, everywhere, as they approached its fine and striking environs, and afterwards drove through those streets which conducted them to the hotel. She was come to be happy, and she felt happy already.'*

And on comparing life in Bath with that in the *'small, retired village'* she came from, Catherine says: *'Here are a variety of amusements, a variety of things to be seen and done all day long, which I can know nothing of there.'*

The game of introductions which Catherine and Henry Tilney engage in is typical of the book's light-hearted approach to the stuffiness of Bath Society:

'Have you been long in Bath, madam?'
'About a week sir.' Replied Catherine, trying not to laugh.
'Indeed! Have you yet honoured the Upper Rooms?'
'Yes, sir, I was there last Monday.'
'And are you altogether pleased with Bath?'
'Yes – I like it very well.'
'Now I must give one smirk and then we may be rationable again.'

4 SYDNEY PLACE

Jane Austen was not averse to engaging in the social diversions which Bath had to offer as long as she was able to withdraw with ease into her more reflective private world. The Austen family's longest residency in Bath was at 4 Sydney Place, and it was here that she was probably at her most settled in the city. Built in 1792 by Thomas Baldwin, a less showy extension of the Pulteney Estate, Sydney Place offered Jane the best of diverse worlds – a short stroll into the fashionable areas of Bath, shopping in Milsom Street, the theatre, the Assembly Rooms, the obligatory promenade along the Royal Crescent on Sunday mornings. But perhaps more importantly to her, the house lay opposite the large pleasure grounds of Sydney Gardens and within easy reach of her favourite country walks.

BEECHEN CLIFF

That noble hill, whose beautiful verdure and hanging coppice render it so striking an object from almost every opening in Bath.

It is from Beechen Cliff, and under Henry Tilney's tutelage, that Catherine Morland is compelled to dismiss the city below as being *'unworthy to make part of a landscape.'*

The view of Bath today from Beechen Cliff

Camden Crescent, where the vain Sir Walter Elliot made his home, in Jane Austen's novel *Persuasion.*

PERSUASION

Persuasion, the second of the two novels which Jane Austen set
largely in Bath, keenly reflects her disenchantment with the city,
exposing in a subtle comedy of manners, the snobbery, vanity and
pretentiousness of much of Bath Society at that time. Catherine
Morland's eager anticipation of her stay in *Northanger Abbey,* is in
marked contrast to Anne Elliot's doleful arrival in *Persuasion,*
where she *'persisted in a very determined, though very silent,
disinclination for Bath; caught the first dim view of the extensive
buildings, smoking in rain, without any wish of seeing them better;
felt their progress through the streets to be, however disagreeable,
yet too rapid.'* Anne Elliot's unwelcome uprooting, mirrors closely,
Jane Austen's own unhappiness at leaving her beloved Hampshire
for Bath in 1801.

Persuasion, written as her health was rapidly failing, is however,
Jane Austen at the height of her literary powers. The novel was
completed only a few months before the close of her short life in
1818.

CAMDEN CRESCENT

The Elliot's fictional residence in Bath is in Camden Place, now
known as Camden Crescent. Built in 1788 by John Eveleigh, who
also designed Somerset Place to the west of Lansdown Crescent,
the steeply sloping site presented many problems to the architect,
and before construction was completed, part of the eastern flank of
the terrace slipped away in a landslide. The crescent remained
unfinished: the intended central pediment, supported on its five
Corinthian columns, is not central at all; there being only four
houses on its eastern side.

Despite its lack of symmetry Camden is a fine terrace,
compensated with spectacular views of the city, particularly on
autumn mornings when the Abbey may be seen rising out of a sea
of mist in the city below.

The pedimented house was most probably the residence of the
Elliots in *Persuasion: 'Their house was undoubtedly the best in
Camden-Place, Everybody was wanting to visit them.'* Sir Walter
Elliot exemplified the new breed of Bath resident: having found
himself in financial difficulties, he moved to Bath as *'It was a much
safer place for a gentleman in his predicament; he might there be
important at comparatively little expense.'* Camden Place provided
him with *'a lofty dignified situation such as becomes a man of
consequence.'* The shaky ground on which Elliot's *'lofty dignified
situation'* was built, provides an irony which Jane Austen almost
certainly intended.

The beauties of nature must be for me one of the joys of heaven.
Jane Austen, from a letter to her sister Cassandra
2nd June 1799

ST. MARY THE VIRGIN CHURCH IN CHARLCOMBE

Jane Austen found relief from the endless round of social events in long walks in the surrounding countryside, spending many hours strolling the hills and valleys around Bath, and visiting nearby villages. One of her favourite walks was to Charlcombe Village and the Norman Church of St Mary the Virgin, where Henry Fielding was married in 1734.

She wrote, in a letter to her sister Cassandra, of the evening of the 31st of May 1799:

We took a very charming walk from 6 to 8, up Beacon Hill and across some fields to the village of Charlcombe, which is sweetly situated in a little green valley, as a village with such a name ought to be.

FANNY BURNEY (1752-1840)

In 1794, When Fanny Burney set out to write her third novel, she had long been out of the literary limelight. She was 42 years old, married to an impoverished French émigré, Alexandre d'Arblay, and the mother of a child not yet a year old. *Camilla, A Portrait of Youth,* was written more in the hope of providing for her family in their straitened circumstances, than to sustain or revive her literary reputation.

The book was sold by advance subscription, a means which gambled heavily on the success of her two earlier novels, *Evelina* and *Cecilia,* to attract readers to pay in advance of publication. One of those who subscribed to *Camilla* – each of whom had their names printed in the first edition – was a Miss J Austen of Steventon, Hampshire. Jane Austen was just 20, and at the start of her own literary adventure, but the names of the two authors would ever be inextricably linked, as much for their associations with, and somewhat different opinions of, Bath, as for the obvious influence, which Fanny Burney's own witty observations of English Society had on her more famous successor.

Unlike Jane Austen, Fanny Burney lived a long and eventful life. She was born twenty-three years before Jane Austen, yet outlived her by a further twenty-three years. It was a life that curiously mirrored the rise and fall of Bath's own fortunes in the late eighteenth and early nineteenth centuries. When she visited the city in 1780, she was still flushed with the early success of her first novel *Evelina* and accepted by the 'Bath circle', as one of the many bright literary and artistic talents who flocked to Bath at the height of its popularity. Thirty-five years later, when she came to live in the city with her husband and son, it was as another of the 'gentile poor' who were now fast occupying the once sought-after Georgian addresses.

The d'Arblays had lived in France after the Peace of Amiens in 1802, hoping to reclaim the property which Alexandre d'Arblay, an army officer loyal to the crown, had forfeited in fleeing the country. At the resumption of war they found themselves trapped and, during the campaigns against Napoleon, Alexandre was seriously injured. Fanny herself witnessed first-hand the horrors of battle. After Napoleon's defeat, she desperately wanted to return to England, where she hoped her husband might regain his former health:

I wish to live in Bath, wish it devoutly, for at Bath we shall live, or nowhere in England. Bath is... the only place for us since here, all the year round, there is always the town at command and always the country for prospect, exercise and delight.

She had her wish, and moved to the city she loved with her family in 1815. But despite her faith in the efficacy of the spa-waters, within three years Alexandre d'Arblay was dead.

Fanny Burney retained an affection for Bath all her life and, though she spent her last years in London, was buried with her husband and their son (whom she also outlived), at St Swithun's Church, Walcot in Bath.

Today, her stature and influence as a writer are once more being acknowledged.

FANNY BURNEY

Among Fanny Burney's many literary accomplishments, were plays, diaries and letters; all of which displayed her trenchant wit and keen observation. One letter, written to her sister Hetty in 1791, contains the following amusing description of the 'rage for building' which gripped Bath in the last decade of the eighteenth century:

This city is so filled with Workmen, dust and lime, that you really want two pair of Eyes to walk about in it, – one for being put out, and the other to see with afterwards. But as I, however, have only one pair, which are pretty much dedicated to the first purpose, you cannot, in reason, expect from me a very distinct description of it. Bath seems now, rather a collection of small Towns, or of magnificent Villas, than one City. They are now building as if the World was but just beginning, and this was the only spot on which its Inhabitants could endure to reside. Nothing is secure from their architectural rage. They build upon the pinnacle of Hills that only to look up to breaks one's neck, – and they build in the deepest depths below, which only to look down upon makes one giddy. Even the streets round the Pump-room are pulling down for new Edifices, and you can only drink from their choice stream, by wading through their chosen mud. Their plans seem all to be formed without the least reference to what adjoins or surrounds them, they are therefore high, low, broad, narrow, long, short, in manners the most unexpected, and by interruptions the most abrupt; – and some of their Houses are placed so zig-zag, in and out, you would suppose them built first, and then dropt, to find their own foundation. They seem seldom to attempt levelling the Ground for the sake of uniformity, but, very contentedly, when they have raised one House on the spot where it could stand most conveniently, they raise the next upon its nearest and steepest activity, so precisely above it, that from the Garret of one, you Mount into the Kitchen of the other.

THE KENNET AND AVON CANAL

At the peak of the canal-building boom in the early
eighteenth century there were over 4000 miles of inland
waterways in Britain. The Kennet and Avon Canal reached
Bath quite late in its short hey-day, joining the River Avon
at the foot of Widcombe Hill in 1810. The prosperity of the
canals was shortlived: within thirty years they were being
superseded by railways as the quicker and more economic
means of passenger and freight transport.

In 1969, after a long period of decay, the Kennet and
Avon Canal Trust began the long task of renovating the
locks and channels, and in 1990 the canal was officially re-
opened as a leisure amenity. In many ways canal-walks
have replaced the pleasant riverside walks of the eighteenth
century, the banks of the Avon having been built up along
much of its approach to the city. The river remains one of
the few natural resources in Bath to have been consistently
undervalued in the last two centuries of town planning.

WILLIAM BECKFORD 1760-1844

One of the most extraordinary characters to have made his home in Bath
was William Beckford. The son of a wealthy sugar plantation owner,
Beckford inherited a vast fortune, which he employed throughout his long
and eventful life, to indulge his diverse and sometimes unorthodox
passions.

A connoisseur of the Arts, he amassed a huge collection of rare books
and manuscripts, paintings, furniture and objets d'art. An interest in the
Orient and the occult was to inspire his own literary claim to fame: the
gothic Arabian novel, *Vathek*, which was published in 1786, and greatly
admired by the poet Byron, who called it a 'sublime tale'. Among his other
accomplishments were travel-writing, poetry, landscape-gardening,
languages and musical composition. At the age of five he had received
music lessons from Mozart – himself only eight at the time. Beckford liked
to refer to Mozart as *'that moonstruck wayward boy'*.

A homosexual scandal in 1784 led to his being more or less ostracised
from English Society for the rest of his life, and the death of his wife in
1786 after giving birth to their second daughter, resulted in a further
withdrawal into his solitary pursuits. Here he remained, embittered and
aloof, for the rest of his life.

He found solace in travel, his vast art collections and the natural
world. He abhorred cruelty to animals, and the gardens that he
landscaped at Fonthill in Wiltshire and in Bath, were designed to
maximise the presence of wild creatures. The twelve-foot high wall he had
built around seven miles of his country estate at Fonthill, was designed
as much to prevent hunting-dogs trampling his land in pursuit of their
quarry to keep out prying neighbours. His family seat is largely
remembered for his other great passion: building. Here he constructed a
magnificent gothic abbey, 312 feet long and 270 feet wide, with a great
central tower 276 feet high. Fonthill Abbey was considered one of the
finest country houses in England.

Debts, arising from his having been cheated out of part of his
plantation revenues, forced him to sell Fonthill and move to Bath in 1822.
At first he considered purchasing Prior Park, but considering it too
expensive, moved instead into the first of three adjacent houses in
Lansdown Crescent he was to purchase, adding an archway at first-floor
level to bridge the narrow lane which divided two of them. Over a period
of time he leased a number of plots of land behind Lansdown Crescent,
which gave him an unbroken strip of garden extending a mile to the top
of Lansdown Hill. Here, 800 feet above sea level, he built a second tower
(a modest 154 feet high), which still stands, and is now usually known as
'Beckford's Tower'. From the top of its narrow, winding staircase, he
would have been able to see – had it still been standing – that other tower
he caused to be built, at Fonthill. A story relates, that on his deathbed,
the contractor responsible for the abbey tower, had confessed to Beckford
that the foundations had not been built to the proper specifications.
Beckford had dutifully passed this message on to its new owner, who
chose to ignore the information, maintaining that as long as it lasted his
own lifetime he did not care. The tower fell in that same year, destroying
most of the abbey – a mere 25 years after its completion.

THE LANSDOWN TOWER

Completed in 1828, Lansdown Tower was designed by H.E. Goodridge, in the Graeco-Roman style fashionable at that time, but with many idiosyncratic touches contributed by Beckford himself.

The interior was furnished with a Crimson Drawing Room, a Scarlet Drawing Room and an Etruscan Library. The Tower is crowned with a gilded lantern, inspired by the Choragic Monument of Lysicrates at Athens.

James Lee-Milne in his biography of William Beckford, described the early-morning visits to the tower that Beckford routinely took in his final years: *Every morning until a few weeks before his death, unless the wind was in the east, when nothing normally induced him to set foot outside the house, Beckford, after drinking a cup of chicken broth, would ride early to the tower. Attended by a cavalcade, preceded by a grey-haired old steward on horseback, then two grooms with long hunting whips. Next rode Beckford with five or six dogs, and in the rear two more grooms with whips...As soon as he reached the tower he would throw his horse's reins to a groom and rapidly climb the Belvedere to admire the panorama.*

He would then wander through the rooms, arrange a bouquet of flowers in a bowl as carefully as if he were painting a still-life, pull out a book from the shelves, read a passage or two, re-arrange the furniture and walk home to breakfast...

This same cavalcade could, on rare occasions, be seen in the streets of Bath with Beckford, the lone eccentric, as oddly out of place in the Victorian city as it is possible to imagine, attracting the curiosity and hushed whispers of the townsfolk.

William Beckford died in 1844 aged 84, and his body lies in a red granite sarcophagus within a moated enclosure at the foot of his tower. The following extract from one of his poems is inscribed on the tomb:

'Eternal power!
Grant me through obvious clouds, one transient gleam of thy bright essence in my dying hour.'

CHARLES DICKENS (1812-70)

By the time Charles Dickens first visited Bath in 1835 as a young reporter for the Morning Chronicle, the city was long past its Age of Elegance, and the sober age of Victorian respectability would soon be as ingrained as the black soot and grime which now covered much of its once honey-coloured walls. A *'grass grown city of the ancients'* is how Dickens himself described it.

On this first visit, he stayed at the Saracen's Head in Broad Street, but it was at another famous hotel and lodging house in Bath, the White Hart Inn in Stall Street, where Dickens has the fictional companions of his first novel stay upon their arrival in the city. The landlord, one Moses Pickwick, also lent his name to the hero and title of the book: *The Posthumous Papers of the Pickwick Club.*

The dowdiness of social life in Bath during the early Victorian era is cleverly satirised in *The Pickwick Papers.* In this extract, Dickens describes a typical evening in the Upper Assembly Rooms:

...In the tea-room, and hovering around the card-tables, were a vast number of queer old ladies and decrepit old gentlemen, discussing all the small talk and scandal of the day...Lounging in the doors, and in remote corners, were various knots of silly young men, displaying various varieties of poppyism and stupidity...And lastly, seated on some of the back benches, where divers unmarried ladies past their grand climacteric, who, not dancing because there were no partners for them, and not playing cards lest they should be set down as irretrievably single, were in the favourable situation of being able to abuse everybody without reflecting on themselves.

In another part of the book, Sam Weller gives his unappealing description of the taste of spa water:

'Have you drank the water, Mr Weller?' inquired his companion, as they walked towards High Street.

'Once,' replied Sam.

'What did you think of 'em, sir?'

'I thought they was particklery unpleasant,' replied Sam.

'Ah,' said Mr John Smauker, 'you dislike the killibeate taste, perhaps?'

'I don't know much about that 'ere, said Sam. 'I thought they's a wery strong flavour o' warm flat irons.'

'That is the killibeate, Mr Weller,' observed Mr John Smauker, contemptuously.

'Well, if it is, it's a wery inexpressive word, that's all,' said Sam.

'It may be, but I ain't much in the chimical line myself, so I can't say.' And here, to the great horror of Mr John Smauker, Sam Weller began to whistle.'

Neither was Dickens much enamoured of some of the steep rows of Georgian houses perched on the precipitous slopes of Lansdown:

A short walk through the city and arrived at the unanimous conclusion that Park Street was very much like the perpendicular streets a man sees in a dream, which he cannot get up for the life of him.

THOMAS A BECKET CHURCH WIDCOMBE

THOMAS A BECKET CHURCH Built by Prior Cantlow on the site of a Saxon chapel and Norman church. The present parish church dates from around 1490.

WILLIAM SAVAGE LANDOR (1775-1864)

When visiting Bath, Charles Dickens occasionally stayed at the home of his friend, the poet and essayist, William Savage Landor, who lived for some years in St James' Square. Dickens is thought to have written much of *Little Dorritt* here, and the irascible poet was himself caricatured - not altogether unsympathetically – as Boythorn in *Bleak House*.

Landor first set eyes on his future wife at a ball in the Assembly Rooms in 1811, remarking to a friend: *'That's the nicest girl in the room and I'll marry her'*. His romantic impulsiveness did not, however, lead to a particularly happy marriage, and the two were separated in 1835. Landor was particularly fond of the parish of Widcombe in Bath, and had hopes of being buried in the tiny churchyard of St Thomas a Becket. In one of his poems he wrote:

'Widcombe! Few seek in thee their resting place, Yet I, when I have run my weary race, Will throw my bones upon thy Churchyard turf'.

Unfortunately, his wish was not to be fulfilled. Financial difficulties resulting from a libel case, forced him to leave the country and settle in Florence, where, in 1858, he died and was buried.

An unusual feature of the stained glass in **St Thomas a Becket Church** is the complete absence of human figures. The window designs feature instead images of shrubs, plants and flowers from the bible.

BATH AFTER THE GEORGIAN ERA

The Georgian era in Bath left behind such an impressive architectural and cultural legacy, that it can be tempting to view much of the century that followed as a postscript to its achievements. But throughout the long Victorian era, Bath would find itself in the grip of profound moral and social changes, which would complete its fall from, favour with wealthy pleasure seekers. The city's cultural life would take a back seat to this drama well into the twentieth century, from which it would emerge rejuvenated and re-energised.

In the early nineteenth century, however, Bath was just making its not always comfortable transition from leisure resort to provincial city of genteel residence. The city's long-simmering social tensions and reputation as a 'Valley of Pleasure', both still deeply entrenched, posed a potential threat to the new image it was attempting to promote.

The widespread discontent with the principles of authority and hierarchy, which had sparked the revolutions of the eighteenth century in Europe and America, had shaken the ruling classes in England.

This discontent found expression in nation-wide disturbances such as the Gordon Riots of 1780, during which Bath saw its share of violent protest. In 1794, Ben Bull, a journeyman tailor in Bath, was imprisoned for illegally distributing copies of the 'seditious' text, *The Rights of Man,* by the English left-wing political writer Thomas Paine. Paine's book advocated such radical ideas as republicanism, deism, the abolition of slavery and the emancipation of women. On its publication, in 1792, Paine was tried, in absentia, for treason. In this climate of political anxiety, Bath, with its notorious social inequalities, was viewed as a potential breeding ground for the new revolutionary fervour.

The city, eager to sustain social harmony, moved to suppress any troubles that might jeopardise its economic future. On the one hand, much was done to relieve the plight of the 'deserving poor'. Charities encouraged an almost feudalistic dependency, in an effort to convince the underclasses that the social order was divined by the Almighty, and that any challenge to this belief was heresy. The 'cheap repository tracts' of the Evangelical pamphleteer Hannah More, who was based in Bath in the 1790s, propounded little short of a 'Divine Right of the Ruling Classes'. A revival of Puritan sentiment once more considered activities such as theatre-going, as dangerous and morally suspect.

The attempts of the Evangelical Church to finally 'dethrone Satan' heralded a period in which almost all the major building projects in the city were for churches. Not surprisingly, Bath lost any remaining vestiges of its reputation as a haven for pleasure-seekers, who now sought 'wanton dalliance' and adventure in warmer climes and freer societies.

BATH AFTER THE GEORGIAN ERA

For a time, the city (like many of its residents) seemed to be dying on its feet. Even the railway, greeted with such enthusiasm when it arrived in Bath in 1841, was to further diminish the tourist trade, as people discovered the English seaside resort. With sea-air, rather than spa-water the new health creed, physicians hastily packed their bags and headed for Brighton and Weymouth.

Attempts to revive the tourist industry in the 1860s, led to plans for a Grand Pump Room Hotel to be built on the site of the old White Hart Inn, which had closed in 1864. The new hotel had only limited success in reviving the fortunes of the tourist industry in the town, but ironically, during demolition of the White Hart, further evidence of the Roman Temple of Sulis Minerva came to light. This would lead to the discovery and excavation of the Roman Baths, now recognised as one of the most spectacular Roman sites in Britain – and one of Bath's biggest tourist attractions.

The Victorian contribution was, despite its unglamorous legacy, a vital one for its future prosperity. The efforts to turn the city into a residential haven for the middle-classes led to improved civic amenities that would benefit all: fresh water supplies, better sanitation, gas and electricity, public parks and libraries, new schools, and improved roads, all helped bring Bath into the modern age, and prepare it for its twentieth-century revival.

LOUIE STRIDE:
THE VOICE OF THE POOR IN EDWARDIAN ENGLAND

Despite these improvements, the plight of the poor remained as intractable as ever well into the Edwardian era. Louie Stride, born in 1907, the illegitimate child of a prostitute, had lived in many of the notorious slums of Bath, including the Holloway and the Dolemeads, or 'mud island' as it was known, due to the fact that it was situated on the low-lying flood plain of the River Avon. Louie Stride's autobiography, *Memoirs of a Street Urchin,* is a poignant reminder of how rarely the voice of the poor was heard. In this extract she describes life as a child in the Dolemeads: *There were some houses quite uninhabitable, in fact some were just rubble...*

We were still in the flood level, and I got used to seeing the gas stove and objects underwater...I grew up scavenging food where I could, in the gutter pretty often, surprising what one can find edible. I ran wild during the day and was locked in at night.

THE BATH ABBEY CEMETERY

One of the major contributions of the Victorian Era was the planned cemetery. These designed landscapes were to provide much needed attractive open spaces at a time when the suburbs were fast consuming the countryside around major cities, contributing, as the poet William Wordsworth had suggested, 'the soothing influences of nature' to the funerary process. In the 1830s a new cemetery was proposed on the southern outskirts of Bath, on land purchased from the Prior Park Estate, to be designed by the architect, social reformer and landscape gardener John Claudius Loudon. The chosen site proved to have been used for similar purposes by the Romans: during landscaping, coffins and skeletons were discovered, as well as Roman coins dating from the time of the Emperor Constantine.

The Abbey Cemetery, consecrated on the 30th January 1844, just a few weeks before his death, remains a perfect testimony to John Loudon's principles of cemetery design: 'Cemeteries, as at present used, ought to be in an elevated and airy situation, open to the north, but with a south aspect, that the surface may be dried in the sun...It should be as near the great mass of the population for which it is intended, as a due regard to their health will permit, in order to lessen the expense of carriage and shorten the time of performance of funerals and of visits by the living to tombs of their friends; it ought to be conspicuous at a distance, from its buildings and tombs. It will generally be an ornament to the surrounding country, and an impressive memento to our mortality.'

Dr James Tunstall in his nineteenth century guide book 'Rambles about Bath', added just a touch of sales pitch to his description of the Abbey Cemetery: 'This City of the Dead boasts scenic surroundings of unusual beauty.'

Bath Abbey Cemetery Chapel designed in Neo-Norman style by the City Architect George Manners. The red granite sarcophagus containing the remains of William Beckford, was first situated in the Abbey Cemetery, before its removal, in 1948, to the newly consecrated ground at the foot of the Lansdown Tower.

THE EMPIRE HOTEL

Later twentieth-century building developments in the city, may have inadvertently done the Empire Hotel something of a favour, by producing any number of new candidates for the-most-hated-building-in-Bath award. The Empire Hotel was built in 1901 to a design by Major C.E. Davis, the City architect responsible for part of the excavation of the Roman Baths a decade earlier. Davis had for years felt his architectural ambitions in the town to have been thwarted, so when he won the commission to build the Empire Hotel, he was obviously intent on making full use of the opportunity to display his powers to the full. The building was once known as 'Major Davis' revenge'.

Its most extraordinary feature – apart from its sheer size – is the roofline, representing the three types of English dwelling: a castle, a manor house and a cottage. Some Bath residents admit to a sneaking affection for the Empire, but there are as many others who still believe it should have been pulled down years ago. It is however, one of the few buildings in Bath to take advantage of its riverside location. The Grand Parade, which leads from the Orange Grove to Pulteney Bridge, is a pleasant walk, with views across the river and to the hills on the eastern fringes of the city.

Beneath the monolithic **Empire Hotel,** in Boat Stall Lane, lies the
Medieval East Gate of the city, which once led to the monk's mill and a
ferry crossing. The area also housed the city's ducking stool – a chair used
for punishing miscreants by plunging them into the river.

Last Reflections: Two more recent 'pilgrims' to Bath were Francis Kilvert and W.H. Hudson. Both men were born in the first years of the Victorian era and both seem to echo the words of more ancient voices; reinforcing the sense of timelessness that Bath can evoke.

FRANCIS KILVERT (1840-79)

The clergyman and diarist, Francis Kilvert, was born in 1840 in Hardenhuish, not far from the city of Bath, which he regularly visited. He died at the age of 39, having produced twenty-four volumes of diaries, only three of which, dating from the last seven years of his life, now survive. His writing shows a sensitive awareness to the landscape of Bath, as these descriptions illustrate:

I think I never saw the beautiful city look lovelier this morning in its early morning's dress, with the blue encircling hills climbed by crescents and terraces and the great Abbey towering above the river and looming across the river meads.
(6th May, 1871)

It was a lovely morning, the clear shining after the rain, and in the strange gauzy sunlit mist of the morning Bath looked like a beautiful mirage with a weird strange unearthly beauty, like an enchanted city.
(8th September, 1873)

The morning was dull, thick and gloomy, threatening rain, but just before we got into Bath a sunbeam stole across the world and lighted the Queen of the West with the ethereal beauty of a fairy city, while all the land blazed gorgeous with the brilliant and many coloured trees. Almost in a moment the dull dark leaden sky was replaced by a sheet of brilliant blue and the lovely city shone dazzling and lustrous upon the hill sides, her palaces veiled with a tender mist and softened by delicate gleams of pearl and blue.
(2nd November, 1874)

W.H. HUDSON (1841-1922)

The novelist and naturalist W.H. Hudson was born in 1841, a year after Francis Kilvert, but his first real literary success came with *Green Mansions,* a novel written a quarter of a century after Kilvert's death.

In the early years of the twentieth century, Hudson travelled widely through England, recording his observations and experiences, much as John Leland and Celia Fiennes had done. The following passage is from his book *Birds and Man,* published in 1901, in which he describes Bath as:

> *...a town of white stone in the hollow of an oblong basin, with the River Avon flowing through it; and though perhaps too large for perfect beauty, it is exceedingly pleasant. Its 'stone walls do not a prison make', since they do not shut you out from rural sights and sounds: walking in almost any street, even in the lowest part, in the busiest, noisiest centre of the town, you have but to lift your eyes to see a green hill not far away; and viewed from the top of one of these hills that encircle it, Bath, in certain favourable states of the atmosphere wears a beautiful look. One afternoon, a couple of miles out, I was on the top of Barrow Hill in sudden, violent storm of rain and wind when the rain ceased, the sun burst out behind me, and the town, rain-wet and sun-flushed, shone white as a city built of whitest marble against the green hills and black cloud on the farther side. Then on the slaty blackness appeared a complete and most brilliant rainbow, on one side streaming athwart the green hill and resting on the centre of the town, so that the high, old, richly-decorated Abbey Church was seen through a band of green and violet mist.*

> *That storm and that rainbow, seen by chance, gave a peculiar grace and glory to Bath, and the bright, unfading picture it left in my memory has perhaps become too much associated in my mind with the thoughts of Bath, and has given me an exaggerated idea of its charm.*

RAINBOWS OVER BENNETT STREET

The early evening light after a heavy storm creates the honey-coloured appearance of the normally white or grey Bath stone.

MODERN TIMES: THE SACK OF BATH

In the Second World War Bath found itself one of the prime targets of Hitler's infamous Baedeker' attacks on British cities of cultural interest.

In three bombing raids which took place on the weekend of the 25th and 26th of April 1942, many buildings in the city were damaged or destroyed and over 400 people lost their lives. Of Bath's major Georgian buildings, the Assembly Rooms was the most severely damaged. The Circus and the Royal Crescent survived (although Nazi propaganda insisted that they had both been partially destroyed). Ironically, greater destruction was to befall Bath's architectural heritage in the peacetime years that followed.

The post-war building boom of the 1950s in war-damaged Britain, fuelled by new and cheaper building materials, easily transported by road and rail, led to an inevitable homogenising of many city developments throughout the country. Bath suffered particularly cruelly in this new 'rage of building' which, with otherwise good intentions, destroyed much of the minor but characterful 18th and 19th century architecture in the city, replacing it with buildings totally out of harmony with its Georgian heritage. In an oft-quoted response to increasing local unease about the devastation, the City Architect at the time was reported to have commented *'If you want to keep Georgian artisans' houses, you will have to find Georgian artisans to live in them.'*

The wanton destruction continued unabated throughout the 1950s and 1960s, until, in 1974, a 'rage *about* building' followed the publication of Adam Fergusson's *The Sack of Bath.* This disquieting study alerted a majority of Bath's residents to the loss of many important aspects of their city's heritage, mourning the demise of:

The city of period architectural vignettes with a myriad tiny alleys and corners and doorways...The set pieces – the Royal Crescent, the Circus, Milsom Street, the Pump Room, and so on – stand glorious and glistening ...But now, more and more because the devastation goes on, they have become like mountains without foothills, like Old Masters without frames.

The impact of the book, together with the tireless work of locals groups such as the Bath Preservation Trust, halted further 'cultural vandalism', and enabled the city to face the challenges of the twenty-first century with at least its central claims to posterity intact.

The Bath Skyline from Widcombe Hill

'A Region that sets Paradise itself before one's Eyes...
The very Elysium Fields of the Antients.'
— John Wood the Elder
from his *'Essay towards a description of Bath'*.

The doom prophesiers of nineteenth-century industrial England, such as William Morris, who had asked bitterly whether all was *'to end in a counting house on the top of a cinder heap, with the pleasures of the eyes having gone from the world'*, have not yet been proved entirely correct. Just as a few passionate and determined individuals helped to preserve the built environment in Bath, so too has much of its natural setting been protected by the efforts of groups such as the National Trust, who today own seven miles of the Bath skyline.

INTO THE TWENTY-FIRST CENTURY

At the dawn of the twenty-first century, the Georgian Era of Bath can seem very far away in time indeed. Its social diversions and bland routines of 'busy idleness' can appear astonishingly dull in comparison with the many opportunities that the modern world has to offer. In fact it is increasingly hard to imagine life in this pre-industrial England – a world that had not yet seen the railway, let alone a car or a plane. When one begins to appreciate the many profound changes the cultural and social revolutions of the nineteenth and twentieth centuries wrought, one can see why, for instance, in the absence of the sophisticated modes of communication which we take for granted, those few available social entertainments required such formal organisation and strict routine.

In some ways our modern world is an inversion of the eighteenth-century experience. We hardly need set foot outside our front doors for most of the necessities, or pleasures, of life, if we choose not to. Ironically, it is the quietude and slow pace of life which our Georgian forbears sought to seek variety from, which has become the rare and precious commodity to us.

The Bath of the twenty-first century is once more a lively, cosmopolitan city. The Palladian buildings are once more gleaming white, and the streets bustle with entertainers, tourists and a thriving residential population. The city still attracts the poor and the dispossessed – persistent reminders of the social inequalities which the city (and society as a whole) has always struggled to balance. It is right that Bath should never feel wholly at ease with these contradictions. Many diverse influences have shaped the character of the ancient city through the ages, but it remains a city with a conscience.

The heritage of Bath is one that offers a chance to reflect on man's achievements, and on his changing relationship with the forces of the natural world he inhabits. The healing springs which drew the peoples of the Stone Age, the Celts, the Romans and countless others since, remain the most consistent of its many claims to posterity, sustaining the city's tradition as a centre of healing and spiritual replenishment, enjoyment and relaxation.

THE THERMAE

When, in her charter of 1590, Elizabeth I gave control of the hot springs to the '*body of citizens and their successors*', it was the Queen's intention that the population of Bath should have access to the healing waters in perpetuity. A promise which the city was able to honour for well over three centuries. But in 1978 a health scare forced the City to close the spa for public bathing. (The cause of the contamination of the springs was not, as some suggested, the revenge of Dr Radcliffe and his poisoned toads!) In time a fresh supply of pure mineral water was tapped from deep below the contaminated spring head, but despite many attempts to re-open them in the years that followed, the baths remained closed to bathers for a quarter of a century.

The thermal waters, however, continued to have their champions. At last with the help of money raised by the Bath Spa Trust, set up in 1977 to aid the advancement of medical research into the springs, an application to the Millennium Commission resulted in funding being made available for a project which would see not only the return of public bathing, but the design and construction of a brand new spa building for the twenty-first century: the New Royal Bath.

The New Royal Bath.

Sir Nicholas Grimshaw and Partners, the architects responsible for the Thermae were faced with the difficult task of designing a modern building which would complement Bath's eighteenth-century architecture - a task which had rarely been successfully achieved in the decades following the 'Sack of Bath' in the 1970s.

The building, essentially a cube of Bath stone enclosed within curvilinear outer screen walls, reflects the design of the Hot Bath. The boundary walls of the Royal Bath, however, differ from Decimus Burton's adaptation of John Wood the Younger's original rectilinear Hot Bath in one important detail: they are made of translucent glass. Features of the spa include an open-air rooftop pool where bathers can enjoy views across Bath's skyline. Spa facilities on different levels of the New Royal Bath include whirlpools, neck massage jets and air-beds, steam rooms, exercise and rest areas, treatment rooms and a restaurant.

The Spa Complex
In addition to the twenty-first century spa building, the Bath Spa Project included faithful restoration of a number of other historic buildings in the area immediately surrounding the two smaller springs. Much of this area had been extensively developed in the late eighteenth century by three great Georgian architects: Thomas Baldwin, John Palmer and John Wood the Younger.

The Cross Bath
The discovery in 1998 of original drawings by John Palmer has led to restoration of the Cross Bath which includes features of his intended designs. Hence the interlocking oval shapes of the pool and the pump room. The Cross Bath is once again a working open-air thermal pool.

The Hot Bath
John Wood the Younger's original design for the Hot Bath contained a central plunge pool surrounded by smaller treatment rooms. This design has been recreated. Twelve medical treatment rooms offer a variety of medical treatments, such as: hydrotherapy, acupuncture and massage.

The Hetling Pump Room
In the eighteenth century the Hetling Pump Room was one of a number of pump rooms in the city where people came to drink the spa water. It was closed in the nineteenth century, when the pump room moved to the Hot Bath. Today it houses a small museum and the spa interpretation centre.

Rooftop view of the Thermae Spa Complex including The Cross Bath, Hot Bath, Hetling Pump Room and St John's Hospital.

Bath Street

Thomas Baldwin's Colonnaded Bath Street links the Pump Room entrance in Stall Street with the Cross Bath and the Thermae complex. This area also includes other important buildings associated with the two smaller thermal springs, including St John's Hospital and the two medieval hospitals of Bellott's and St Catherine's. Numbers 7/7a and 8 Bath Street in the south-west corner have been renovated to serve functions related to the Thermae Bath Spa.

Spa culture may once again thrive in the city to a degree that it has not done since the city's Georgian hey-day and not perhaps in such comfort since the glory days of the Roman Aquae Sulis.

8 Bath Street

Known as the 'House of Antiquities', 8 Bath Street was once a museum storing the archaeological findings uncovered in the city during the eighteenth-century redevelopment of the Pump Room. The weathered statues of King Edgar and the mythical King Coel once stood in niches above fishmongers' stalls in the seventeenth-century Guildhall.

The Rooftop Pool and Bath Abbey

Behind the modern spa building the Medieval Abbey presents a stark contrast until perhaps one considers that the surface of the abbey itself is said to be 4/7th glass, and is sometimes called the 'Lantern of the West'.

CAM HOBHOUSE

Perhaps some future pilgrim to the ancient city of
Bath will find nothing but the ruins of its glorious
past, as one Saxon monk recorded many centuries
ago in his poem, *'The Ruin'*. This time it may be the
remains of the Circus or the Crescent which are held
in awe; the ingenuity and imagination of its ancient
authors marvelled at. Cam Hobhouse, in *'The
Wonders of a Week at Bath'*, published in 1811, may
already have provided us with such an elegy,
reminding us that all things must perish – even Bath.

BUT, ALAS! what can Time the destroyer withstand?
Where's Troy? where's the May-pole,
*   that rose in the strand?*
E'en thou, noble city! must perish, and if
Beacon Hill shall shake hands with his
*   friend Beechen Cliff,*
(As a prophet foretold, and fixing the day,
Drove all true believers in terror away,)
Then with no slow-consumption,
*   but swallow'd entire,*
Thy mirth and thy music at once shall expire.
All at once shall be crush'd both the old and the young
Of all who so caper'd, and all who so sung,
Of Square, Crescent, Circus, no traces remain,
And the valley of Bladud be turn'd to a plain.
Yet still on that plain the green surface shall show
Some signs of the Wonders once working below;
For still shall thy streams of hot water be found,
Still the caverns return no unmusical sound;
And the shepherd shall swear, whilst attending his
flock,
That he hears us a footing it under the rock...

THE CIRCUS PLANE TREES

A winter sunset provides a stunning backdrop to the silhouetted plane trees towering high above the rooftops of the Circus.

CHRISTOPHER ANSTEY

But perhaps the last word should go after all to
Christopher Anstey and the spirit of Georgian Bath.
After all, it is largely to pay homage to the
extraordinary endeavours of Beau Nash, John Wood
and Ralph Allen, that millions are still drawn from
around the world to the city of white stone in the
Valley of the Sacred Spring.

A FAREWELL TO BATH

Paid bells, and musicians,
Drugs, nurse, and physicians,
Balls, raffles, subscriptions, and chairs;
Wigs, gowns, skins, and trimming,
Good books for the women,
Plays, concerts, tea negus and prayers.

Paid the following schemes,
Of all who it seems
Make charity – bus'ness their care:
A gamester decay'd,
And a prudish old maid
By gaiety brought to despair;

A fiddler of note,
Who for lace on his coat,
To his taylor was much in arrears:
An author of merit,
Who wrote with such spirit
The pillory took off his ears.

...Farewell then, ye streams,
Ye poetical themes!
Sweet fountains for curing the spleen!
I'm griev'd to the heart
Without cash to depart,
And quit this adorable scene!

Where gaming and grace
Each other embrace
Dissipation and piety meet
May all, who've a notion
Of cards or devotion,
Make Bath their delightful retreat!

The New Bath Guide 1776

Further Reading

As with most Bath guide books aimed at a general readership this one owes a considerable debt to the primary historical research undertaken in the city by dedicated enthusiasts and historians. There have been so many books written about Bath (including some good ones sadly out of print) that researching a particular aspect of its history can be a daunting task for the interested reader. The following books represent a selection of the writings from each of the critical periods in Bath's history that I found particularly helpful during my own research for this book. I have given the most recent editions wherever possible.

Barry Cunliffe	*Wessex to AD 1000*; Longman, London; 1993
	Roman Bath Discovered; 3rd ed. Tempus, Stroud; 2000
Peter Davenport	*Medieval Bath Uncovered*, Tempus, Stroud; 2002
Edith Sitwell	*Bath*; Redcliffe, Bristol; 1983
Trevor Fawcett	*Voices of Eighteenth Century Bath*; Ruton, Bath; 1983
Oliver Goldsmith	*The Life of Richard Nash*; Newbery, London; 1762
David Gadd	*Georgian Summer*; Countryside, Newbury; 1987
Neil Jackson	*Nineteenth Century Bath*; Ashgrove Press, Bath; 1998
RS Neale	*Bath: A Social History, 1680-1850*; RKP, London; 1981
G Davis and P Bonsall	*Bath: A New History*; Keele University Press; 1996
A Fergusson and T Mowl	*The Sack of Bath*; Michael Russell, Salisbury; 1989.
Tim Mowl	*John Wood, Architect of Obsession*; Millstream, Bath; 1988
	William Beckford; John Murray, London; 1998
Maggie Lane	*A City of Palaces*; Millstream, Bath; 1999
Louie Stride	*Memoirs of a Street Urchin*; Bath University Press; 1984
Walter Ison	*The Georgian Buildings of Bath*; Kingsmead, Bath; 1980
Bryan Little	*The Building of Bath*; Collins, London; 1947
Thom Gorst	*Bath: An Architectural Guide*; Ellipsis, London; 1997
Christopher Pound	*Genius of Bath*; Millstream, Bath; 1987

For a fascinating insight into the mind of architect John Wood the Elder, try his *Essay Towards a Description of Bath* (Kingsmead, Bath, 1969). Not always easy reading, but intriguing none the less. For some interesting and unusual insights into Bath's architectural history, *A Window on Bath* (Millstream Books, Bath, 1994) by Kirsten Elliot is excellent, particularly for the keen walker.

Bath Abbey and the Entrance to the Roman Baths